The Infinite Way

By

JOEL S. GOLDSMITH

Third Edition
1949

★

Martino Publishing
Mansfield Centre, CT
2011

Martino Publishing
P.O. Box 373,
Mansfield Centre, CT 06250 USA

www.martinopublishing.com

ISBN   978-1-61427-127-7

Cover design by T. Matarazzo

Printed in the United States of America On 100% Acid-Free Paper

The Infinite Way

By

JOEL S. GOLDSMITH

Third Edition
1949

★

WILLING PUBLISHING COMPANY
251 S. San Gabriel Blvd.
San Gabriel, California

Printed in the United States of America
by Willing Publishing Company
San Gabriel, California

DEDICATED

To you
To whom this already belongs

There is no need to run outside
For better seeing,
Nor to peer from a window. Rather abide
At the center of your being;
For the more you leave it, the less you learn.

LAOTZE

Truth is within ourselves.
There is an inmost center in us all,
Where the Truth abides in fulness; and to
*   know*
Rather consists in opening out a way
Whence the imprisoned splendor may escape
Than in effecting entry for a light
Supposed to be without.

ROBERT BROWNING

A god has made his abode within our breast:
when He rouses us, the glow of inspiration
warms us; this holy rapture springs from the
seeds of the divine Mind sown in man.

OVID

Most men take a problem, not to themselves,
not into the chambers of their own minds, but
to the first directory of persons whom they
can consult.

VALDIVAR

The kingdom of God is within you.

JESUS

INTRODUCTION

Sitting before a blank sheet of paper and wondering what I was going to say by way of introduction to this book which I know so well, leafing its pages in search of some line or passage which might cue me to a start, I found my thoughts turning away from its contents to the essential mystery of my profession as a writer—the mystery of where they would be coming, those words that I was going to put down, which are already these words that I *am* putting down. I need hardly say that this was not the first time that I had asked myself that question; it confronts me each time that I find myself with no idea of what I am going to write next, causing me to ask where they have *all* come from, all those many thousands of words and thoughts that I have in the past put down on paper, to be reproduced in print or on the stage. It is the sort of question that one is apt to ask only in such moments of frustration; for the most part we

take for granted these things that are in fact the daily miracles of life, as we take for
3 granted the miracle of growth and germination, scattering seeds in a garden and never being surprised that from those tiny black
6 specks next summer's flowers can be relied upon to come.

That attitude is one for which G. K.
9 Chesterton was always rebuking the world, for taking its mysteries and its miracles as a matter of course. It is the theme of his too
12 little known fantasy "MANALIVE," whose hero was in a state of continual amazement at the miracle of living, and was so eager
15 to keep that amazement alive that he travelled around the world in order to recapture the excitement of coming home to his own
18 house and his own front door, and courted, eloped with and remarried his own wife under six different names, so as never to lose
21 sight of the incredible wonder of love.

It is our tragedy that we live so in a state of acceptance, and yet the essentials of daily
24 living seem to demand it if we are to get on with our business and our work. I use the word "seem" quite deliberately, for, actu-

ally, the truth, I think, is just the opposite, and what has been called "the rich, full life" is impossible on such a basis. Even an 3 ordinary, humdrum life is difficult. Its mechanics have a way of breaking down, and the hard facts of opposition and mischance 6 a way of turning into brick walls against which one butts one's head in vain. It is in those moments that men start asking themselves 9 questions about the world they live in, and to look for some explanation, help or sustenance. Religion, the conventional 12 forms of religion, involving a personal God to whom petitionary prayers are addressed, is apt to prove fruitless and to lead to no 15 more than a pious, gloomy resignation, and the philosophy of pure materialism, an acceptance of "that is the way things are," 18 leads only to a cursing despair.

Something else is needed; has always been needed, and has always been there to 21 find, though it would seem that man has almost always missed it. It has eluded him through all the writings of the seekers of 24 the truth about the eternal mystery, from orientals such as Lao-Tse and Shankara, through Jesus, the mediaeval European mystics and the thinkers of the New World. Essentially, they have all taught the same things, which is why Aldous Huxley has named his anthology of religious thought, "The Perennial Philosophy." But always the answers, as they have been revealed, have remained somehow apart, "out there," set off from man in his daily life and the facts of his daily living, so that there has grown up a kind of unfortunate snobbery on the subject, as though it were somehow vulgar to expect tangible or practical results, and man has been forced into a fatal dualism, trying to live on two planes at once, the material and the spiritual, both apparently equally real, yet without any understandable relation to each other, like a firm composed of two partners who are not on speaking terms. That is where, I think, this book goes further, removing that duality, showing the two partners to be one only, so that the world becomes one, and the eternal truths a part of the very fabric of our daily life, enhancing its harmonies and erasing its discords.

INTRODUCTION

What is this book? Readers today want labels, want to know what it is they are buying. But they are apt to be put off by labels, too, which is why I find myself in a difficulty if I try to anticipate that question in relation to this work. Half the world, though it is desperately in need, and even in conscious need, of an answer to its problems, will not open a book that it is told is a religious one. Give it a title such as "How to Get More Health, Wealth and Happiness," and though an enormous public will buy it, the fastidious and discriminating will avert their heads from it as from a bad odor. Use the word "metaphysics," and it has a chilly, intellectual sound; present it as a volume of essays and we have the reason why Emerson is read almost exclusively as literature today, instead of for his answers to the same questions. Can one ever by any one road reach all men? The very word "God" is a deterrent to many. It is all over this book. The instinct that I have to apologize for it is an illustration of my problem in writing this foreword.

If it is hard to label the book, it is harder

still to label the author. Who and what is
Joel Goldsmith? A teacher? A healer? They
3 are suspect and off-putting words at best, to
all but a very few, and they are words, too,
that I cannot but feel the author himself
6 would vigorously repudiate, since his whole
philosophy is the denial of any personal ele-
ment in either teaching or healing. I am re-
9 minded of a passage in this book. "Always
there have appeared men bearing the divine
message of the presence of God, and the
12 unreality of evil. . . . (who) brought the
Light of Truth to man, and always men
have interpreted this Light as the Messen-
15 ger, failing to see that what they were beholding as a man 'out there' was the Light
of Truth within their own consciousness."

18   Let me therefore leave both the man and
the book for a moment and return to my
starting point. In moments of trouble and
21 frustration, man begins to ask questions,
even if only such questions as "Why does
this have to happen to me?" or "How can I
24 stop this happening?" He looks for an explanation of what the world is about. I believe he will find it here. He hopes that this

explanation will act somehow as a cure for
his troubles. I believe, too, that if he under-
stands it aright, it will. But here again I 3
must sound a note of warning. In the very
first pages he will find a paradox which may
frighten him. He comes to this quest with a 6
human problem, in the hope of a solution
for it. He is told that if he wants to use
Spiritual Truth to improve human condi- 9
tions, it neither can nor will do so. He is
shown logically why it cannot. But he is
told, too, that if he seeks that Truth for its 12
own sake, his human conditions will be improved. It sounds like something out of a
fairy story, some defeating injunction laid 15
by a quibbling wizard upon a magic wish.
But the point about fairy stories is that their
basis is so often universally true. There is a 18
legend about an alchemist who promised to
turn any substance into gold, provided that
no one in his audience thought about a blue 21
monkey. The point might be improved by
substituting the condition: "Provided that no
one in the audience thought about the gold." 24
It sounds impossible. But it can be done. It
must be done. "Seek ye first the kingdom of

God and His righteousness, and all these things shall be added unto you." But you
3 must not think about those other things.

The point of this book is that it teaches you to look away from your problems in-
6 stead of at them, and in doing so to find their solution, just as in looking away from the problem of what I was going to write in this
9 introduction, I have found myself writing it, good or bad. It is not an easy task that it of- fers, but I think it is an essential one. I think
12 that without some understanding of what this book is about, life is just not quite worth living.

JOHN VAN DRUTEN.

AUTHOR'S NOTE

There is a *way* whereby we are able to rid ourselves of sin, sickness, poverty and the results of wars and economic changes. This *way* is the exchanging of our material sense of existence for the understanding and consciousness of life as spiritual.

Down the centuries, the sense of man and the universe as being material has resulted in the development of fear for the personal self and national existence. This will continue and become even more intensified as more destructive material forces are discovered. (The latest announced is one ounce of a chemical which, it is claimed, is sufficient to destroy the entire population of the United States and Canada). This is probably not even the ultimate of material force. There is no material power to overcome either this or the atomic bomb. There is no hope in matter or material sense. The *way* of security, harmony and health is through attaining some measure of spiritual consciousness.

The Great Secret is that despite all belief to the contrary real power, either for good or evil, does not reside in matter or in the material sense of man and the universe. Those who have acquired some degree of spiritual consciousness have proven in that measure the reality of Spirit.

The necessity for giving up the material sense of existence for the attainment of the spiritual consciousness of life and its activities is the secret of the Seers, Prophets and Saints of all ages. That it is practical is proven today by the healing and regenerating works done by many students of modern schools of practical or scientific Christianity. When the world learns that whatever success has been gained in improving conditions of health, wealth and security in the lives of these modern followers of ancient Teachings has been accomplished solely by the surrender of material sense through attainment of spiritual consciousness, it may well look up with hope.

The Question is, "How does one set about to attain this spiritual consciousness and thereby lose the material sense?" The An-

swer is, "Read and study the truths revealed
through all ages about the universal Mind,
Soul or Spirit and about spiritual creation 3
and its laws. Imbibe the spiritual sense of
these Revelations."

In this small volume, I have written the 6
spiritual truth as I have gleaned it through
over thirty years of study of the major re-
ligions and philosophies of all ages, the last 9
fifteen years of which have been spent in the
practical application of Truth to problems
of human existence — problems of health, 12
business, family life and security.

Be assured inner peace will come as one
turns to the spiritual consciousness of life 15
and an outer calm will follow in one's human affairs. The outer world will conform
to the inner awareness of Truth. 18

The authority for all of this Revelation
will be you — as you yourself experience this
change within and without. 21

CONTENTS

PUTTING ON IMMORTALITY

"**I**N THE BEGINNING was the Word, and the Word was with God, and the Word was God . . . and the Word was made flesh. . . ." 3

"The Word was made flesh"—but it still is the Word. By being made flesh it does not change its nature, character or substance. 6 Cause becomes visible as effect, but the essence or substance is still the Word, Spirit or Mind. 9

In this wise do we understand that there is not a spiritual universe and a material world, but rather that what appears as our 12 world is the Word made flesh, or Spirit made visible, or Mind expressed as idea.

All the error that has existed down the 15 ages is founded on the theory or belief of two worlds, one the heavenly Kingdom, or spiritual Life, and the other a material world 18 or mortal existence, each separate from the other.

In spite of this sense of two worlds, men 21

have always attempted to bring harmony
into the discords of human existence through
3 an attempt by prayer to contact this other
world or spiritual realm and to bring Spirit
or God to act upon the so-called material
6 existence.

Let *us*, then, begin with the understanding
that our world is not an erroneous one, but
9 rather that the universe in which we live
is the realm of Reality about which man en-
tertains a false concept. The work of bring-
12 ing health and harmony into our experience
is not, then, getting rid of or even changing a mortal material universe, but in cor-
15 recting the finite concept of our existence.

The seeker of Truth starts his search with
a problem — perhaps with many problems.
18 The first years of his search are devoted to
overcoming discords and healing disease
through prayer to some higher Power or the
21 application of spiritual laws or Truth to
these mortal conditions. The day arrives,
however, when he perhaps discovers that the
24 application of Truth to human problems
either does not "work" or does not work as
it once did, or else he finds there is now less

of satisfaction and inspiration in his study. Eventually he is led to the great revelation that mortals only put on immortality as 3 mortality disappears — they do not add immortal spiritual harmony to human conditions. God does not create, nor does He con- 6 trol material affairs. "The natural (human) man receiveth not the things of the Spirit of God" for "they are spiritually discerned." 9

Are we seeking "the things of the Spirit of God" for some human purpose, or are we really endeavoring to "put off" the mortal 12 in order that we may behold the harmony of the spiritual realm?

While we strive and struggle and contend 15 with the so-called powers of this world, combating sickness and sin, or lack, spiritual sense reveals that "My kingdom is not 18 of this world." Only as we transcend the desire to improve our humanhood do we understand this vital statement. When, how- 21 ever, we leave the realm of human betterment, we catch the first glimpse of the meaning of "I have overcome the world." 24

We have not overcome the world while we are seeking to have less of the world's

pains and more of the world's pleasures and profits. And if we are not overcoming
3   the sense of struggle over worldly affairs, we are not entering the realm of heavenly affairs.

6   "For whatsoever is born of God overcometh the world." Spiritual Consciousness over-comes the world — both the pains and
9   pleasures of the world. We cannot accomplish this evangelization of humanhood by mental might or physical power, but by the
12 spiritual sense of existence which all may cultivate through devotion of thought to things of the Spirit. "For all that is in the
15 world, the lust of the flesh, and the lust of the eyes, and the pride of life, is not of the Father, but is of the world." Here is the
18 guide. Watch your thoughts, aims and ambitions for just a short while and see if your mind is on your health, pleasures of the
21 senses, or worldly gain. Then as these worldly thoughts appear, learn to reject them because now we are no longer set on
24 the path of improving our human affairs, but on attaining the spiritual kingdom.

"Love not the world, neither the things

that are in the world. If any man love the world, the love of the Father is not in him." Does this sound as if we were becoming 3 ascetic? Do we appear now to be desiring a life apart from the normal, joyous, successful walks of life? Do not be deceived. 6 Only those who have learned to keep their attention on spiritual things have tasted the full joys of home, companionship and suc- 9 cessful enterprise. Only those who have in a measure become centered in God have found safety, security and peace right in the 12 midst of a war-torn world. Spiritual sense does not remove us from our normal surroundings, nor does it deprive us of the love 15 and companionship so necessary to a full life. It merely places it on a higher level where it is no longer at the mercy of chance 18 or change or loss, and where the spiritual value of the so-called human scene is made manifest. 21

"Labour not for the meat which perisheth, but for that meat which endureth unto everlasting life." "For the kingdom of God is 24 not meat and drink; but righteousness, and peace, and joy in the Holy Ghost."

When confronted with any human problem, instead of laboring for an improved human condition, turn from the picture and realize the presence of the divine Spirit in you. This spirit dissolves the human seeming and reveals spiritual harmony, though to sight this harmony will appear as improved human health or wealth. When Jesus fed the miltitude it was his spiritual consciousness of abundance that appeared as loaves and fishes. When he healed the sick, it was his feeling of the divine Presence that appeared as health, strength and harmony.

This may all be summed up in Paul's words — "Set your affection on things above, not on things on the earth."

We are living in a spiritual universe, but the finite sense has set a picture before us of limitation. While thought is on the picture before us — "this world" — we are engaged in the constant effort to improve or change it. As soon as we lift our vision — take thought off what we shall eat and drink and wear — we begin to behold spiritual Reality which appears to us as improved beliefs, but which really is more-appearing of Reality. This more appearing Reality brings with it joys untold here and now; pleasures 3 beyond our wildest imagination and the love of all with whom we come in contact, even the love of those who do not know the 6 source of the new life we have discovered.

"Peace I leave with you, my peace I give unto you; *not as the world giveth,* give I 9 unto you."

"Now we have received, not the spirit of the world, but the spirit which is of God 12 . . . Which things also we speak, not in the words which man's wisdom teacheth, but which the Holy Ghost teacheth. . . . But the 15 natural man receiveth not the things of the Spirit of God: for they are foolishness unto him: neither can he know them, because 18 they are spiritually discerned."

How often do we go on the rocks on this point! How frequently we attempt to un- 21 derstand spiritual wisdom with our human intellect! This leads to mental indigestion. We are attempting to digest spiritual food 24 with our educated mentality. It will not work. Truth is not a reasoning process,

therefore it must be spiritually discerned. Truth does not as a rule appeal to our rea-
3 son. When it appears to do so, we must search deeply to see if it really is Truth. Be suspicious of a truth that seems reasonable.
6 Jesus walking on the water, feeding the multitudes with a few loaves and fishes, healing the sick and raising the dead — does
9 all this seem reasonable to you? If the Principle underlying these experiences was understood through reason, all the churches
12 would be teaching them as present possibilities and they would recommend their practice. But this Principle is apparent only
15 to spiritual sense and this cultivated spiritual consciousness can do the things that the Christ has ever done. What was possible to
18 Christ consciousness then is possible to that same consciousness now.

We now are engaged in the cultivation of
21 that spiritual sense and we shall succeed in proportion as we relax our mental struggle and become receptive to those things which
24 the Spirit of God teaches. Instead of trying to make Spirit operate upon our human bodies and material affairs, let us learn to

disregard these mortal pictures and keep our vision on things above. When we "come down to earth again" we shall find the dis- 3 cords and limitations of sense have disappeared and more of Reality appearing.

The kingdom of God does not consist of 6 more and better matter nor does it necessarily include a greater vocabulary of Truth. Yet the fruitage of spiritual understanding is 9 greater harmony, peace, prosperity, joy and more ideal companionships and relationships.   12

"For this cause also thank we God without ceasing, because, when ye received the word of God which ye heard of us, ye re- 15 ceived it not as the word of men, but as it is in truth, the word of God, which effectually worketh also in you that believe" (un- 18 derstand).

To receive the word of God or spiritual sense, we need to feel rather than reason. 21 This is referred to Biblically as receiving the word "in the heart." Note here that the development of the spiritual consciousness 24 results in a greater gift of feeling the harmony of being. We understand that neither

seeing, hearing, tasting, touching nor smelling will reveal spiritual Truth or its har-
3   monies to us; therefore, it must come
through a different faculty, the intuitive faculty which acts through feeling. Heretofore
6   we have sat down to pray or to meditate and
immediately a stream of words and thoughts
started to flow. Perhaps we began to affirm
9   Truth and deny error. You can see that this
is wholly in the realm of the human mind.
In cultivating our spiritual sense, we become
12   receptive to thoughts which come to us
from within. We become hearers of the
Word rather than speakers. We become so
15   attuned to Spirit that we feel the divine harmony of being; we feel the actual presence
of God. Having transcended the five phys-
18   ical senses, our intuitive faculty is alert, receptive and responsive to the things of the
Spirit and we begin our new existence as a
21   result of this spiritual rebirth.

Heretofore we have been concerned with
the letter of Truth; now only with the Spirit
24   of Truth. We are not so concerned now with
what is Truth as with feeling Truth. This is
accomplished in proportion as we give less

thought to the letter and more receptivity to the feel. This word "feel," incidentally, refers also to awareness, consciousness, or 3 sense of Truth. We are not now speaking Truth but receiving Truth. That which we receive in silence we may speak from the 6 housetops with authority.

Spiritual healing is the natural result of a divinely illumined consciouness. We are 9 illumined only as we are receptive and responsive to spiritual illumination.

We misunderstand immortality when we 12 think of it as the immortality of the human personality, or personal sense. Death does not produce immortality or end personal 15 sense, neither does the continuation of human existence mean the attainment of immortality. 18

Immortality is attained in proportion as personal sense is overcome, whether here or hereafter. As we put off the personal ego 21 and attain the consciousness of our real self — the Reality of us, divine consciousness — we attain immortality. And that can be 24 achieved here and now.

The desire to perpetuate our false sense of body and wealth ensnares us into death, or mortality.

The first step in the attainment of immortality is living *out* from the center of our being, as in the idea of unfoldment from within, rather than accretion; it is the *giving* sense rather than *getting; being* rather than *attaining.* In this consciousness there is no condemning, judging, hating or fearing, but rather a continuous feeling of love and forgiving.

It is not a simple matter to show forth the joy and peace of immortality, because to those intent on preserving their present concepts of being, immortality would appear to be extinction. This is not the case; it is the eternal preservation of all that is real, fine, noble, harmonious, gracious, unselfish and peaceful. It is *Reality* brought to light in place of the illusion of sense. It is the conscious awareness of the infinity of individual being replacing the finite sense of existence.

Selfishness and conceit fall away in the realization of the divinity of our being.

This realization brings forth patience and

forbearance with those still struggling in mortal, material consciousness. It is being *in* the world but not *of* it.

3

SPIRITUAL ILLUMINATION

Spiritual illumination enables us to discern the spiritual reality where the human concept appears to be. Material sense sees what it believes and then believes what it sees. Spiritual sense discerns the reality of that which is appearing as concept.

The development of spiritual consciousness begins with our first realization that what we are beholding through sight, hearing, tasting, touching and smelling, is not the reality of things. Disregarding appearances entirely, the first ray of spiritual illumination brings us hints of the divine, the eternal and immortal. This in turn makes the appearance even less real to us, thereby admitting even greater illumination.

Our progress Spiritward is in proportion to the illumination which enables us to behold more and more of Reality. Because the human scene is entirely misconception through misperception, any thought of helping, healing, correcting or changing the material picture must be relinquished in order that we may see the ever-present Reality. 3

Spiritual illumination has come to us in a measure with our first investigation of Truth. We believed that we were seeking 6 good, or Truth, whereas the Light was beginning to shine in our consciousness compelling us to take the steps we have since 9 taken. Every increase of our spiritual understanding was more Light appearing and dispelling the darkness of sense. This inflow of 12 illumination will continue until we come to the full realization of our true identity as "the light of the world." Without illumi- 15 nation we struggle with the forces of the world; we labor for a living; we struggle to maintain our place and position; we com- 18 pete for riches or honors. Often we war with our own friends and even find ourselves at war with ourselves. There is no security in 21 personal possessions even after the battle to acquire them has been won.

Illumination brings first peace, then con- 24 fidence and assurance; it brings rest from the world's contests and then all good flows

to us through Grace. We see now that we
do not live by acquiring, gaining or achiev-
3 ing. We live by Grace; we possess all as the
gift of God; we do not get our good, we already have all good. "Son, . . . all that I
6 have is thine."

The pleasures and successes of the world
are as nothing compared with the joys and
9 treasures which now unfold to us through
spiritual sense. In the light of Truth the
greatest earthly happiness and triumph is as
12 nothing, whereas the treasures of Soul have
a glory unknown and unfathomed by sense.

Possessing the divine Light within him,
15 man gains his freedom from the world and
security from all earthly or human dangers.
This period holds terrors and fears for many.
18 The spiritually illumined will recognize
that because no good can come or go; that
because spiritual activity is always of the
21 nature of fulfillment; that because their
illumination has revealed the reality of
things, they are anchored in Soul, in God-
24 consciousness, in spiritual peace, security
and serenity.

We will fear no change in the outer picture because the outer is but the reflection of the allness within. Safe in the realization that we are individual though infinite 3 spiritual consciousness embodying all good, we need give no consideration to the evidence of the senses. 6

Spiritual illumination reveals the harmony of being and dispels the evidence of material sense. It does not change anything 9 in the universe for this is a spiritual universe peopled with children of God, but the illumination changes our concept of the uni- 12 verse.

This is but the beginning of this vast subject. While we are on it, let us keep 15 thought removed as far as possible from the world of sense and anchored in the conscious awareness of spiritual Reality. 18

Always there have appeared men bearing the divine message of the presence of God and of the unreality of evil. Buddha 21 of India; Laotze of China; Jesus of Nazareth; these and many others brought the Light of Truth to men, and always men 24 have interpreted this Light as the Messenger, failing to see that what they were beholding as a man "out there" was the Light of Truth within their own consciousness.

3   In worshipping Jesus men lost the Christ. In devotion to Jesus men failed to apprehend the Christ. In seeking good through 6 Jesus men failed to find the omnipresent Christ in their own consciousness.

   In every case, the Messenger appearing to 9 man is the advent of the Christ in individual consciousness and when so understood, freedom from personal sense and personal limi- 12 tation has been attained.

   Jesus said, "If I go not away, the Comforter will not come unto you." Was this 15 not clear enough for all to understand? If you do not look away from the personal sense of salvation, mediation and guidance, 18 you will not find the great Light within your own consciousness.

   Spiritual illumination does not come from 21 a person, but from the impersonal Christ, the universal Truth, the illumined consciousness of your Self.

24   Illumined consciousness dispels the personal sense of self with its problems, ills, ages, and failures. It reveals the real Self,

the I that I am, unlimited, unfettered, un-
troubled, harmonious and free. This Selfhood is revealed as we retire within our-   3
selves each day and there learn to "listen"
and to watch. Likewise, instead of anxious
care about the work of the day or the events   6
of the future, we let the Soul or our divine
Spirit go ahead of us to smooth and prepare the way; we let this divine Influence   9
remain behind us to safeguard every step
from the illusions of sense.

Illumined consciousness always knows   12
that there is an infinite, all-powerful Presence prospering every act and blessing every
thought. It knows that all who touch us on   15
life's highway must feel the benediction of
our thought.

When consciousness is afire with Truth   18
and Love it destroys all sense of fear, doubt,
hate, envy, disease and discord — and this
pure consciousness is felt by all whom we   21
meet and it lightens the load they carry. It is
impossible to be "the light of the world" and
not dispel the darkness of those about us.   24
Realize that all the good you experience is
the shining forth of your own consciousness

even when it appears to come from or through some other individual. Recognize
3 every evil appearance as a false perception of harmony and therefore not to be feared or hated, and this will result in the disap-
6 pearance of the illusion and the showing forth of Reality. Only illumined conscious-ness can look upon an evil appearance and
9 perceive the divine Reality. Only the Christ in consciousness can strip error of its seem-ing reality and rob it of its sting.

12 Spiritual illumination reveals that we are not mortals — not even humans — but that we are pure spiritual Being; divine Con-
15 sciousness; self-sustaining Life; all-inclusive Mind. This light destroys the illusions of personal sense.

18 Illumination dissolves all material ties and binds men together with the golden chains of spiritual understanding; it ac-
21 knowledges only the leadership of the Christ; it has no ritual or rule but the di-vine, impersonal universal Love; no other
24 worship than the inner Flame that is ever lit at the shrine of Spirit. This union is the free state of spiritual brotherhood. The only

restraint is the discipline of Soul, therefore we know liberty without license; we are a united universe without physical limits; a 3 divine service to God without ceremony or creed.

The illumined walk without fear — by 6 Grace.

To know that we are the fulfillment of God; that we are that place in consciousness 9 where God shines through, is to be spiritually minded. The realization that every individual is the presence of God; that all 12 that is, is God-appearing, is spiritual consciousness. The understanding that what we see, hear, taste, touch or smell through the 15 five physical senses is but the finite concept of Reality and in no wise related to the spiritually real, is spiritual sense. 18

Christ Consciousness beholds God everywhere shining through the mist of personal sense. It recognizes no sinner to be re- 21 formed, no sick to heal, no poor to enrich. Spiritual illumination dispels the false concepts or images of finite sense and reveals 24 all being as God-appearing.

The Light in individual consciousness reveals the world of God's creating, the universe of Reality, the children of God. In this Light, the mortal scene disappears; the world of concepts, "this world," gives place to "My kingdom"—the reality of things seen as they are.

Likewise, there is always the sense of an inner companionship. We feel an inner warmth, a living presence, a divine assurance. Sometimes we feel a strong hand in ours or behold a smiling face over our shoulder. We are never alone and we know it. This sweet Presence gives us an inner Rest; it enables us to relax from the strain of the world and brings us the joy of Peace. In Truth, it is a "Peace, be still," to every problem or strain of human existence. It is a healing influence within us and yet it is felt by all those about us.

This inner Presence of which we are aware is Truth itself interpreting itself to us as Presence, Power, Companion, Christ, Light, Peace and Healing Influence. The consciousness of this inner Being is the result of our greater spiritual illumination, of our cultivated spiritual consciousness. This

Truth is the "God who healeth our diseases" and it goes ever before us to make smooth our path in life. This Truth is wealth and 3 appears as our abundant supply. No human circumstance or condition can lessen our income and wealth while we abide in this con- 6 sciousness of the presence of Love.

Establish this Truth within you and it becomes your real Being, knowing neither birth 9 nor death, youth nor age, health nor disease — but only the eternality of harmonious being. This Truth dispels every illusion of 12 sense and reveals the infinite harmony of your being. It dispels mortality and reveals your immortality. Whatever in your thought 15 is unlike this divine Presence, Truth itself, must yield in order that you may drink the pure Water of Life and eat the spiritual 18 Meat of Truth.

To free our hearts from the errors of self — self-will, false desires, ambitions and 21 greed — is to reflect the Light of Truth as the perfect diamond reflects its own inner light. 24

About 500 B. C. it was written: "It easily happens that a man, when taking a bath,

steps upon a wet rope and imagines that it is a snake. Horror will overcome him, and
3 he will shake from fear, anticipating in his thought all the agonies caused by the serpent's venomous bite. What a relief does
6 this man experience when he sees that the rope is no snake. The cause of his fright lies in his error, his ignorance, his illusion. If
9 the true nature of the rope is recognized, his tranquility of mind will come back to him; he will feel relieved; he will be joyful
12 and happy. This is the state of mind of one who has recognized that there is no personal self, that the cause of all his troubles, cares
15 and vanities is a mirage, a shadow, a dream."

So again, illumination reveals that there is no error; that what appears as the snake
18 — sin, disease, discord, death — is Reality itself misperceived by finite sense. Then discords are not to be hated, feared, or resented,
21 but reinterpreted until the true nature of the rope — Reality — is discerned through spiritual sense. The snake (disease or dis-
24 cord) is a state of mind merely, with no corresponding external reality. It must be

understood that no illusion is or ever can be externalized.

Spiritual illumination may be attained by 3 living constantly in the consciousness of the presence of perfection; by the continual translation of the visible picture into the 6 Reality. We are being faced with discordant appearances all through our days and nights. These must immediately be translated 9 through our understanding of the "new tongue," the language of Spirit. Every incident of our daily experience offers fresh 12 opportunities to use our spiritual understanding. Each use of the spiritual faculties results in greater spiritual perception, which 15 in turn reveals more and more of the Light of Truth. "Pray without ceasing." "And ye shall know the truth, and the truth shall 18 make you free." Translate the pictures and incidents of daily existence into the new tongue, the language of Spirit, and con- 21 sciousness will expand until translation occurs without even taking thought. It becomes an habitual state of consciousness, a 24 constant awareness of Truth.

Only in this wise can we find our lives

unfolding harmoniously from the center of
our being without taking conscious thought.
3 Instead of our existence being a continual
round of "demonstrations," it becomes the
natural, harmonious, joyous unfoldment of
6 good. Instead of repeated efforts to make
good come to us, our every good unfolds to
view without conscious effort, either physi-
9 cal or mental, from the depths of our own
being. We are no longer dependent on
person or circumstance, nor even on our
12 personal effort. Spiritual illumination enables us to relax our personal efforts and
rely more and more on divinity unfolding
15 and revealing itself as us.

THE CHRIST

ANCIENT Scripture reveals: "Hard it is
to understand: By giving away our food, we
get more strength; by bestowing clothing 3
on others, we gain more beauty; by found-
ing abodes of purity and truth, we acquire
great treasures." 6

Abraham, the Hebrew Father, founded
the prosperity of his people on the idea of
tithing — giving a tenth of one's income to 9
spiritual or charitable purposes without any
thought of repayment or reward.

"The immortal can be reached only by 12
continuous acts of kindliness, and perfection is accomplished by compassion and
charity." The greater the degree of unselfed 15
love that we attain, the nearer we come to
the realization of the universal "I" as our
real being. 18

The personal sense of I is busily engaged
in getting, achieving, desiring, accomplishing, accumulating, — whereas our real Self 21

is giving, bestowing, sharing, blessing. The personal sense of self is the embodiment of
3 all human experiences, most of which are limited and undesirable; the real Self is the embodiment of infinite spiritual ideas and
6 activities forever expressing itself without limit or restraint.

The small I concerns itself primarily with
9 its personal problems and affairs, enlarging its borders to include members of the immediate family or circle of friends. The per-
12 sonal sense often goes further afield into charitable works or community welfare; and we know that it is personal sense when
15 we analyze the motives which govern. The real sense of Self lives out from the center of its being, blessing all whom it touches
18 and is recognized by its selflessness; by its unselfishness; by its lack of seeking recognition, reward, or any personal aggrandize-
21 ment. It is not a spineless entity or a floor-mop to be pushed around by mortals — it is never seen or known by mortals.
24 Two beautiful illustrations come to mind revealing in tender scenes the difference be-

tween the personal self and the immortal real Self.

Siddartha had left his home and family 3 in search of Truth, finally received enlightenment and became Buddha, or the Enlightened One, or as we term it, the Christ 6 of his day. His father, a great King, was about to die and, desiring to see his son, sent, asking him to return. When he sat 9 face to face with his son he realized that he had lost him in the personal sense of father and son, but tried nevertheless to reclaim 12 him. "I would offer thee my Kingdom," said the King, "but if I did, thou wouldst account it but as ashes." And Buddha said, 15 "I know that the King's heart is full of love . . . but let the ties of love that bind you to the son whom you lost embrace with equal 18 kindness all your fellow beings, and you will receive in his place a greater one than Siddartha; you will receive the Enlightened 21 One, the Teacher of Truth, the Preacher of Righteousness, and also the Peace of God into your heart." 24

The other concerns the great Master. "While he yet talked to the people, behold,

his mother and his brethren stood without,
desiring to speak with him. . . . But he an-
3 swered and said unto him that told him,
Who is my mother? and who are my
brethren? And he stretched forth his hands
6 toward his disciples, and said, Behold my
mother and my brethren! For whosoever
shall do the will of my Father which is in
9 heaven, the same is my brother, and sister,
and mother."

In proportion as we become spiritually
12 illumined, we are sought out by those seeking freedom from phases of material darkness — sickness, sin, limitations, fear, un-
15 rest or ignorance. We are able to meet these
needs only as we impersonalize both good
and evil, and understand that harmony is
18 the quality and activity of Soul, universally
and individually expressing itself.

In meditation or communion, we become
21 receptive to Truth unfolding within us —
and this we term prayer. Our prayer should
not be connected with a so-called patient.
24 Actually, prayer is not a process, a com-
bination of words or thoughts; nor statements, declarations, affirmations nor denials.

Prayer is a state of consciousness in which we experience the realization of harmony, perfection, oneness, joy, peace and domin- 3 ion. Often, prayer or communion brings to the individual some specific truth and this truth appears outwardly as the fruitage of 6 our own consciousness of real being.

It has been revealed times without number that the talent, ability, education and 9 experience of every individual is actually Mind unfolding itself in individual ways — as artist, musician, salesman, business man, 12 actor. It follows therefore that Mind, thus expressing itself is never without opportunity, recognition and reception. Thus there 15 can be no unrecognized gift, no unexpressed talent or ability, no unrewarded effort, since *all* effort and action is Mind expressing its 18 infinite capacities and capabilities. The conscious awareness of this truth would result in dispelling the illusion of unemployment, 21 lack of compensation or appreciation. Yet — and mark this well — the recitation of these words without some measure of the 24 "feel" of this truth would be as "clouds without rain" — "vain repetition," nothingness.

3 In this same manner, it has been revealed that as there is but one Life, this One is never in danger of sickness, accident, or
6 death. This Life is the Life of individual being. It is never necessary to direct a treatment at a person or an animal, but always
9 to be alert and never accept any suggestion in thought of any other presence, power, or activity than that of the one Life, one Mind,
12 one Soul. To live constantly in this consciousness of good, of harmony, would dispel the illusion of sense whether appearing
15 as sick or sinful person. The declaration or constant affirmation of this truth would avail us but little, whereas the conscious
18 awareness or feel of it would appear as healing or reformation, renewal and even resurrection.
21 Recently I wrote a friend on the occasion of his birthday and I know he will be glad for me to share with you the ideas that came
24 as I wrote:

"As for birthday wishes, I shall just wish that you didn't have any birthdays so that you could get used to the idea of the continuity of conscious existence without a break or a stop — a conscious awareness of pro- 3 gressive unfoldment.

"Truly there is no break in the continuity of unfolding consciousness; nor can con- 6 sciousness lose its conscious awareness of body any more than you can lose your consciousness of the developed musical or 9 artistic or other talent you possess.

"Consciousness unfolds from within to the without from a boundless basis or 12 source; from the infinity of your being to the individual awareness of it in infinite variety, form and expression. 15

"Death is the belief that consciousness loses its awareness of its body. Immortality is the understanding of the truth that con- 18 sciousness is eternally aware of its own identity, body, form or expression. Consciousness aware of its own infinite being 21 and eternal body is immortality achieved here and now. The awareness of consciousness maintaining its own identity and form 24 is eternal life. The awareness of consciousness forever unfolding in individual forms

of creation or manifestation is immortality demonstrated here and now. This conscious-
3 ness is you."

Spiritual consciousness is the release from personal effort in the realization that har-
6 mony is. This consciousness with its release from personal effort, is attained as we find the Christ within us a present Reality. The
9 Christ is the activity of Truth in individual consciousness. It is not necessarily declarations of Truth so much as the reception of
12 Truth. As we attain an inner stillness we become more and more receptive to Truth declaring itself to us, within us. The activity
15 of this Truth in our consciousness is the Christ, the very presence of God. Truth received and continuously entertained in our
18 consciousness is the law of harmony to all our affairs. It governs, guides, leads, directs and supports our every activity of daily ex-
21 istence. Where a belief of illness or lack may be, this ever-present Truth becomes our Healer and Supplier, yes, our Health and
24 our Supply.

To many the word Christ persists as a more or less mysterious term, an unknown entity, something rarely if ever experienced by them. This we must change if we are to benefit by the revelation of Christ Jesus and many others, of a divine presence or power within us. We must experience the Christ as a permanent and continuous dispensation. We must live in the constant conscious awareness of Truth active within. Maintain always a receptive attitude within — a listening ear — and soon you will experience an inner awareness. And this is the activity of Truth in consciousness, or the Christ attained.

This understanding of the Christ clarifies the subject of prayer for us. The dictionary explanations of prayer all conform to a concept of prayer which is based on the erroneous belief that there is a God waiting somewhere for you to pray to it in some manner. Then, if you find this God in the right frame of mind, you might have your prayers answered favorably. Unless, of course, your parents or grandparents for three or four generations back have sinned, in which case you will be held accountable for their sins and your prayer will go into the wastebasket of heaven.

3   We have a different sense of prayer. We realize that whatever of good comes to us, is the direct result of our own understand-
6   ing of the nature of our own being. Our understanding of spiritual life unfolds in proportion to our receptivity to Truth. Not
9   praying up to Mind, but *letting* Mind unfold and reveal itself to us. This is the higher concept of prayer. It is achieved as
12   we take a few minutes now and then during the day and evening to meditate, commune, listen. In quietness we become a state
15   of receptivity which opens the way for us to feel or become aware of the very presence of God. This feel or awareness is the activ-
18   ity of God, Truth, in our consciousness — it is the Christ, the Reality of us.

Ordinarily we live in a world of sense
21   and concern ourself only with the objects of sense. This gives us our experiences of good and evil, pain and pleasure. As we, through
24   our study and meditation, turn more to the mental side of life, we find that we develop higher thoughts and therefore we experi-

ence better conditions. As our mental qualities become more refined, and we take on
more patience, kindness, charitableness, 3
forgiveness, our human experiences reflect
these qualities back to us. But let us not
stop there. 6

Higher even than the plane of body and
mind, there is the realm of Soul, the kingdom of God. Here we find the Reality of 9
our being, our divine nature. Not that body
and mind are separate or apart from Soul,
but that Soul is the deepest recess of our 12
being.

In the realm of Soul we find complete
tranquility; absolute peace, harmony and 15
dominion. Here we find neither good nor
evil, pain nor pleasure, only the joy of being.
We are in the world but not of it because 18
we no longer see the world of sense as it
appears to be but, having awakened our
spiritual sense, we "see Him as He is," — 21
we see through appearances to the Real.

Ordinarily we have sought our happiness
in the objective universe, in person, place or 24
thing. Now, through spiritual sense, Soul
sense, the whole world tends to bring its

gifts to us — though no longer through desire for person or thing, but merely through
3 the avenue of these. In material sense person and thing are the objectives of our sense — that which we desire. Through Soul
6 sense, our good unfolds from within us though appearing as person and improved condition. Soul sense does not deprive us of
9 the friends and family and comforts of human existence, but brings them more surely to us on a higher and more beautiful and
12 permanent level of consciousness.

For many centuries attention has been centered on Jesus Christ as the Saviour of
15 man, and during these centuries the spiritual sense of life has fluctuated from one extreme to another of light and darkness. A
18 sixteenth century teacher writes: "Christ (Jesus) calls Himself the Light of the world, but He also tells His disciples that
21 *they* too are the Light of the world. All Christians in whom the Holy Ghost lives — that is, all real Christians — are one with
24 Christ in God and are like Christ (Jesus). They will therefore have similar experiences,

and what Christ (Jesus) did, they will do also."

Our task is the realization of the Christ 3 of our own consciousness. We acknowledge with joy and deep love the measure of the Christ attained not only by Jesus, but by 6 many spiritual seers and prophets of all ages. Our hearts are filled with gratitude for the measure of the Christ manifested by so 9 many men and women of today. We now look forward to the realization of the Christ of our own consciousness. "The kingdom 12 of God is in you and he who searches for it outside himself will never find it, for apart from God no one can either seek or find 15 God, for he who seeks God, already in truth has Him."

We must understand the word conscious- 18 ness, because we can only prove what we are conscious of. Where do we stand in con- sciousness? Are we still mortals? Or have 21 we renounced our material selfhood and acknowledged ourselves to be the Christ, the fulfillment, the presence of God? Some 24 day we must give up the effort to get, and acknowledge ourselves to be the eternal

Giver in action. We must feed five thousand without taking thought as to whence it shall

3 come. Out of our Christhood the multitudes may be supplied. Wherein then is lack except in the belief that we are humans? We

6 must give up this belief and claim our true identity.

When we are confronted with any person

9 or circumstance that appears to be mortal we must realize "Thou art the Christ, the Son of the living God" and all that appears

12 mortal is illusion or nothingness. We will fear no mortal and no material circumstance because we recognize its nothingness.

15 Truth is simple. There are no deep metaphysics nor mysterious truths. It is either Truth or not Truth, but there cannot be

18 deep Truth and shallow Truth; nor can there be degrees of Truth. Truth to be Truth must be absolute Truth. We are con-

21 cerned now with the truth that we individualize infinite power. We must not look to a power outside of or apart from ourselves.

24 We individualize infinite power in proportion to our consciousness of Truth.

The Life which is God is your life. There

is but one Life and this is the life of all being, of every individual. You individualize
this eternal Life and it is no less God in one   3
than in another, and it is diseaseless and
deathless in all. Our consciousness of this
truth is the healing influence within us.   6

There is but one Mind, God. You individualize this omnipotent, omniscient Mind —
therefore your mind is the ever-present help   9
in every circumstance. For this reason you
do not pray to or contact some far-off
Mind but realize the omnipresence of di-   12
vine Mind as your mind, and let go of the
seeming problem. The awareness of this
truth establishes you in the consciousness of   15
the presence of Mind, Life, Truth, God.
The understanding of the oneness of Mind
as your mind, of Life as your life, is Truth   18
eternal.

The next step in unfoldment is the realization that as the individualization of Mind   21
you embody within your own consciousness
your body, your business, home. You can
only prove your dominion over the weather,   24
climate, income, health and body as you
know these to be ideas in the mind or con-

sciousness which you are. These ideas, home, employment, body, are ideas within you and

3 subject to your understanding and the consciousness of this truth gives you dominion. This does not exalt humanhood or make it

6 divine. It wipes out humanhood and reveals the divinity of you.

We can measure our spiritual unfold-

9 ment by watching whether or not we are trying to improve the physical scene. We must remember that the structural life of man,

12 animal or plant is not the one Life, God, but the human, limited concept of real Life; therefore any attempt to heal, change or

15 correct the physical universe is evidence that we have not developed sufficient spiritual consciousness.

18 Christ Consciousness recognizes all life to be God — but realizes that what appears to material sight and sound is not that life

21 but merely the illusion or false sense of existence. Spiritual consciousness discerns the life which is real.

24 As we cannot meet a problem on the level of the problem, we must rise above the level of appearance in order to bring out the

harmony of being. That which is visible to the five senses is not the reality of things — therefore we cannot think from that level. 3 Disregarding appearances, we turn from the picture before the senses and begin there to become aware of Reality — of that which 6 eternally is.

OUR REAL EXISTENCE

Our real existence is as Spirit. Some seekers may not understand what we mean by this. Only in the degree that we perceive our real existence as Spirit, do we drop the false sense of life as material. Then we see that the structural life of man, animal and plant is but the false sense of existence; that our concern for the so-called necessities of material living has been unnecessary; that though the beauties we behold all hint at God's creation, they are not that spiritual and perfect creation; that the sick, aging, dying appearances are not at all a part of real life; then only do we begin to catch glimpses of eternal spiritual existence untouched by material conditions or mortal thoughts. As we turn from the world we see, hear, taste, touch and smell, we catch inspired visions which show forth the earth of God's creating.

In healing work we must turn from the

structural universe we see. We must remember that we are not called upon to heal
it, change it, alter it, correct it or save it. 3
We are first of all to realize that it exists
only as illusion, as the false sense of life.
From this vantage point in consciousness we 6
behold through spiritual sense the "house
not made with hands, eternal in the
heavens." 9

We are apt to think of certain persons as
good providers, good earners, good sales-
men, good healers. Let us understand this 12
correctly. It is never a person but a state of
consciousness which heals, regenerates,
paints, writes or composes. The state of con- 15
sciousness becomes visible to us as a person
because of the finite concept we entertain
of God and man. We often suffer disap- 18
pointment when some people fail to live up
to the picture we have formed of them.
This is because we have ascribed the good 21
qualities of consciousness to person — then
when a person fails to live up to those qualities we have erroneously believed to be 24
him or her, we suffer.

In the Bible we meet with the characters

Moses, Isaiah, Jesus, Paul. We should realize that Moses represents the Leader state
3 of consciousness or Leadership; Isaiah presents to us Prophecy; Jesus shows forth the
Messiah consciousness or saving and heal-
6 ing Grace; Paul carries the consciousness of
the Messenger, Preacher or Teacher. Always, however, it is the particular state of
9 consciousness expressing itself and appearing to us as men.

George Washington was certainly the
12 consciousness of national integrity; Abraham Lincoln the consciousness of individual
integrity and equality.

15 When we think of ourselves let us forget
our so-called humanhood and human qualities and try to understand what we represent
18 as consciousness and then realize that that
consciousness which is expressing itself as
us is likewise maintaining and prospering us
21 and our endeavors.

Failure often comes through the belief
that we express God, or Life, or intelligence;
24 or that we express God qualities. This is
never true. God, Mind, is forever expressing itself and its qualities. Mind, Life,

Spirit, can never fail. Our task is to learn to relax and *let* our Soul express itself. Egotism is the attempt to be or do something through either personal physical or mental effort. To "take no thought" is to refrain from conscious thinking and let divine ideas fill our consciousness. Since we are individual spiritual consciousness we can always trust that consciousness to fulfill itself and its mission. We are the spectator or witness of this divine activity of Life expressing and fulfilling itself.

More and more we must become the spectator or witness. We must become the Beholder of Life and its harmonies. Each morning we should awaken with eagerness to watch the new day unfolding and revealing each hour new joys and victories. Several times each day we should consciously realize that we are witnessing the revelation of Life eternal; the unfolding of Mind and its infinite expression; the activity of Spirit and its grand formations. In every situation of our daily experience let us learn to stand back of ourselves and see God at work, witness the play of Love upon our affairs, watch

God reveal Himself in all those about us.

Every night we should realize that our
3 rest does not bring to a close God's activity
in our experience, but that Love is the protecting influence and substance of our rest;
6 that Mind is imparting its ideas to us even
in sleep; that Principle is the guiding law
throughout the night. Nothing from with-
9 out can enter consciousness to defile, and
this truth stands guard at our mental portals
to admit only Reality and its harmonies.

12 Be a Beholder, a Witness. Watch the
unveiling of the Christ in your consciousness.

15 There is a constant warfare between the
flesh and the Spirit and this will continue as
long as we entertain any degree of corporeal
18 sense. The attempt to bring Spirit and its
laws to bear upon material concepts constitutes this war, and peace can only come
21 when the structural sense of the universe
and the corporeal sense of man has been
overcome.

24 Notice how often you try to apply some
metaphysical truth to a human problem and
you will discover the reason for the conflict

within you. Our goal actually is the attainment of spiritual harmony rather than continuing in a material sense of existence with 3 more ease or comfort.

In the early days of our search for Truth we probably had no other thought beyond 6 making a sick body well, or a poor person more affluent, or reforming a sinning man into a moral one. No doubt that in turning 9 to a practitioner or teacher of spiritual consciousness, we seemed to achieve this end and for some time we continued to "use" 12 Truth or God to govern our material concept of man and the world. It is only as we continue in our spiritual studies and medi- 15 tation that we eventually become aware of an inner conflict. We enjoy moments of mountain experiences; we tumble into the 18 valley of uncertainty; we achieve victories and then experience failure; we alternate between apparent good and evil, success and 21 failure, spirituality and mortality, health and illness. This is the inner conflict that becomes evident as the warfare between the 24 flesh and the Spirit. This will only end as we drop the mortal or corporeal sense and

achieve the consciousness of spiritual existence.

3   "My kingdom is not of this world" is the
foundation for the building of the new and
higher consciousness. The willingness and
6 ability to look away from the human sense
of person and thing and perceive the man
and universe of God's creating is essential.

9   Gaining more dollars is not spiritual supply; greater savings does not constitute
security; physical health is not necessarily a
12 foundation for eternal life. These constitute
improved human belief.

    The advancing student will gradually re-
15 linquish his attempts to improve humanhood or to improve beliefs in order that the
truth of spiritual existence may unfold in
18 his consciousness.

    The spiritual realm is the source of health
which is truly eternal harmony of being; it
21 is a consciousness of supply without limits
and gained without taking thought. Remember, however, that we are not again
24 connecting God, or Spirit, with the human
sense of health and supply. We are rather
coming into the awareness of spiritual

health and supply. Heretofore our efforts have been in the direction of manifesting greater harmony and dominion in our earthly affairs. That this consciousness of heavenly being seems to result in more harmonious human living is true, but these are the "added things" which follows the seeking of heaven and its righteousness. The heavenly sense of righteousness will be found to be far different than the human concept of goodness, and it is this higher sense of good we should seek.

"My thoughts are not your thoughts, neither are your ways my ways." For this reason we are not attempting to think more or better human thoughts nor to have our human ways made more smooth. We truly are seeking to learn God's thoughts and God's ways.

At this state of unfoldment we realize the need of dropping all concern for ourselves and for our own welfare. We are learning that concern for our personal welfare is building on sand, whereas a life devoted to the search for Truth is a foundation of rock upon which we may build the eternal

Temple of Life. Lasting happiness and prosperity is found when we have a Principle or
3 Cause to which we can devote ourselves. We are now finding less of self in our existence and thereby making room for the
6 revelation and unfoldment of our divine Self. In this Self we discover our completeness and the infinity of our being. Here
9 also we discover the reason for our existence.

God evolved the world and all that is
12 therein. What we behold through sense is not that world but is the false and finite concept of the world of God's creating.
15 Rising in consciousness we begin to perceive the spiritual universe and something of its purpose.

18 He who has found his inner self realizes that he is one with all men, animals and things. He knows now that what affects one
21 touches all; that what blesses one blesses all. The universality of this truth is found in all Scripture, as you will note in these
24 examples:

*Let one conquer the mean man by a
gift. Charity is rich in returns; charity*

*is the greatest wealth, for though it
scatters, it brings no repentance.*

HINDU SCRIPTURE 3

*Theirs was the fulness of heaven and
earth; the more that they gave to
others, the more they had.*

CHINESE SCRIPTURE 6

*And give unto him who is of kin to
you, his due, and also unto the poor,
and the traveller. And what good ye
have sent before your souls, ye shall
find it with God.* TURKISH SCRIPTURE 12

9

*It is more blessed to give than to re-
ceive. . . Give, and it shall be given
unto you; good measure, pressed down,
and shaken together, and running over
shall men give into your bosom. For
with the same measure that ye mete
withal it shall be measured to you
again.* THE BIBLE

15

18

As we realize our unity or oneness with 21
all creation, we become more loving, gentle,
patient, understanding. Then only are we
fulfilling the great teaching "Love thy 24

73

neighbor as thyself" and then only are we glimpsing the kingdom of God — "the Temple not made with hands" — the man and universe of God's creating. It is this spiritual man, the man of God's creating, who has been given dominion over all the earth.

There is no mystery about the inner Life except the mystery of Godliness. Every thinker is concerned for his welfare; the welfare of his family; community; for his country or even for the world. Experience soon convinces him that there is no hope for mankind in the people or the powers of this world. Men are too selfish. On the whole they are too concerned for their own interests to be wholly unselfish in their attitude toward the world.

The more ambitious are often endowed with greater physical or mental attainments and soon sit in the seats of the mighty, and the world is led by those lacking in integrity and love. Politicians rarely rise any higher than self-seeking. The occasional statesman is lost in the picture.

Here and there in the world there are

those inspired men and women who long for the dawn of the day of the Brotherhood of Man. Their hearts ache at the constant 3 ridicule of men of good will and at the ever-recurring success of the power-drunk or money-mad in each succeeding generation. 6 These noble people of vision are buffeted between their hope for the progress of mankind and the realization of the futility of 9 overcoming the forces of evil operating in human thought. Eventually the same question comes to each one: Is there no power to 12 stop this reign of evil; to halt wars; prevent famine and pestilence? Is man helpless before the Four Horsemen? 15

The search for freedom from the trials and tribulations of human experience has begun. It is really a search for God and it 18 begins at whatever place in consciousness the individual may find himself. If he has a deep religious sense with a church back- 21 ground, he may seek the Power in religious worship, in some creed or dogma or some particular form of worship. The intellectual 24 will undoubtedly seek the Power in the realm of philosophy or one or another of

the philosophical religious teachings. In more recent times the search may turn to the
3 metaphysical church teachings or oriental Yoga practices. Without doubt many go from one to another of these steps still seek-
6 ing God or the Power which may eventually halt the reign of mortality. One day something happens within. Consciousness ex-
9 pands and sees that which before was invisible. One "feels" a glow of warmth; a Presence never before known becomes tangible,
12 very real. This often is a fleeting experience. One may not even be certain that it occurred. It lingers in memory, but more as a dream
15 than an actuality, until it happens again, and this time more clearly, more definite and perhaps lasting longer. Gradually there
18 dawns in consciousness the realization of a Presence always present. This Presence may be felt as if lurking in the background of
21 one's consciousness. At times it becomes a very commanding Presence dominating the scene or experience of the moment.
24 Now, however, evil is becoming less real; sickness is not so acute; financial stress or even lack gradually gives way to sufficiency;

concern for one's self disappears as every need is met without taking thought or planning or worry or fear. The people or powers 3 which heretofore have been feared now fade from view and either disappear from one's experience or else are seen for their power- 6 lessness. Desires become less acute. Fears evaporate. Assurance, confidence, alertness, keeness, these become evident not only to 9 one's self but to those who are met and dealt with in everyday life.

The inner Presence has likewise become 12 an inner Power. From an occasional experience it has become the constant awareness. Forces of pain and pleasure in the outer ex- 15 perience diminish whereas one becomes conscious of inner powers which are real and which produce and govern the outer life 18 harmoniously and fruitfully. There is no longer fear of the evils of the outer world, nor is there the intense pleasure in the hap- 21 pier things of the outer world. It is possible to have the pleasures of the world and enjoy them; or not to have them and not miss 24 them. There is a constant joy within that needs no outside stimulus.

In this consciousness, God is found to be the inner Light or at least this Light is felt as an emanation of God. God is felt as a divine Presence or Influence within. It is felt by those who come in contact with the man who has found his inner Self. It is reflected in his health and success. It radiates from him as sunbeams radiate from the sun.

In finding his inner Life, this man has found peace, joy, harmony, security. Even in the midst of a failing world he stands unmoved, untouched — the very presence of immortal Being.

When we are no longer limited by the five physical senses and have attained even a measure of spiritual sense or Christ Consciousness, we find ourselves unlimited in terms of "here" or "there," "now" or "hereafter." There is a going in and coming out without sense of time or space; an unfolding without degree; a realization without an object.

In this Consciousness finite sense disappears and the vision is without boundaries. Life is seen and understood as unfettered form and limitless beauty. Even the

wisdom of the ages is encompassed in a
moment. Death disappears and once more
we see those previously separated from us 3
by this so-called impassable barrier. This
communion is not the communication of
spiritualism but an awareness of eternal life 6
untouched by death. It is the reality of immortality seen and understood. It is a vision
of life without beginning and with no end. 9
It is Reality brought to light. In this Consciousness there are no physical barriers of
time and space. The vision encompasses the 12
universe. It bridges time and eternity. It includes all being.

In this light we see without the eye; we 15
hear without the ear; we understand things
not known before. Where we are, God is,
because there is no longer separation or di- 18
vision. Here there are no rewards and no
punishments. Harmony is. Life is not dependent on processes; we do not live by 21
bread alone. (*I have the sense of "peeking"
into heaven and seeing what mortal eyes
were not meant to see*). 24
Spiritual sense is not engaged with human good and yet this Christ Consciousness

reveals the harmony of being in what appears as our human experiences and in
3 forms available to our present circumstance. Though "my kingdom is not of this world," yet "your Father knoweth that ye have need
6 of these things" and He supplies your wants even before you ask.

And he said unto his disciples, There-
9 fore I say unto you, Take no thought for your life, what ye shall eat; neither for the body, what ye shall put on.

12 The life is more than meat, and the body is more than raiment.

Consider the ravens: for they neither
15 sow nor reap; which neither have storehouse nor barn; and God feedeth them: how much more are ye better
18 than the fowls?

And which of you with taking thought can add to his stature one cubit?

21 If ye then be not able to do that thing which is least, why take ye thought for the rest?

24 Consider the lilies how they grow: they toil not, they spin not; and yet I say

unto you, that Solomon in all his glory was not arrayed like one of these.

If then God so clothe the grass, which 3 is today in the field, and tomorrow is cast into the oven; how much more will he clothe you, O ye of little faith? 6

And seek not ye what ye shall eat, or what ye shall drink, neither be ye of doubtful mind. 9

For all these things do the nations of the world seek after: and your Father knoweth that ye have need of these 12 things.

But rather seek ye the kingdom of God; and all these things shall be 15 added unto you.

Fear not, little flock; for it is your Father's good pleasure to give you the 18 kingdom.

Luke 12:22-32

SOUL

THE SOUL is a part of man which is little known and only seldom realized.

3   Often those in the depth of some deep sorrow break through the mist of material sense to the recesses of their inmost being;

6 here they discover the Soul or Reality of being. They become Soul-conscious, and find new values, new resources, new and dif-

9 ferent strength, and an existence of an entirely different nature.

  The exercise of the Soul faculties results

12 in breaking the illusions of sense. All human discords are products of material sense and are experienced through the five physi-

15 cal senses — that is, all mortal inharmonies are seen, heard, felt, tasted or smelled. Existing only in this material state of con-

18 sciousness, discords, disease, etc., have their being merely as false sense or illusion, though naturally seeming very real to the

21 senses.

SOUL

There are many means of securing temporary relief from erroneous conditions of health, wealth, and other inharmonies of   3
daily existence. Complete and final destruction of error comes only through the achievement and exercise of the faculties of   6
the Soul. The Soul is that part of man which lies buried deepest within him and is therefore seldom realized. We use our mathe-   9
matical faculties and our musical faculties because these lie nearest the surface of our being. Much more than these, even, are our   12
ordinary business faculties; our sense of direction, or even an artistic sense. Artists and authors and skilled musicians go deeper   15
within their being and bring forth the great harmonies of fine music, classical writings, paintings, sculpture and architecture.   18

Hidden even deeper than these, yet within the reach of our own consciousness, lies the Soul and its faculties. These Soul pow-   21
ers, when touched by us, come forth from within us and reach every avenue of our daily living, giving inspiration, beauty,   24
peace, joy and harmony to each moment of our existence and clothing every event in our

experience with love, understanding, success.

Those so busy with the pains and the
3 pleasures of sense will not, of course, reach
the realm of Soul. Throughout the ages the
invitation has been extended to mankind to
6 drink of this fountain of living waters, and
every generation has produced many men
and women who have found eternal youth
9 and peace within themselves. Ever so often
one arises who has drunk more deeply at
the fount of Soul and these seers have told
12 of the kingdom within and of the life that
may be lived through grace when this consciousness is achieved. So many answer that
15 they have great human duties to occupy all
their time; others require so much time for
sense pleasures, pastimes and recreations;
18 still others are immersed in accomplishing
and acquiring.

More and more, people are beginning to
21 realize that freedom from fear, insecurity,
want, and ill health is not to be found in the
material realm. Wars will not end wars;
24 investments will not insure security from
want; medicines alleviate pain but do not
produce real health.

SOUL

Some greater power must be tapped to give us the happiness and harmony and peace that is our birthright, than can be found in the human body or thought. This power is available to everyone because it is already a part of our being — in fact, it is the greatest part of our being. As the iceberg reveals only a portion of itself in sight above water, so our human powers of body and mind represent not more than one-third of our powers and faculties.

The powers of the Soul are more real and tangible than any of the material powers of nature or invention. They operate on a higher level of consciousness but are made evident in so-called human affairs.

Soul forces act upon the human body to produce and maintain health and harmony. They touch every avenue of daily existence as protective influences and are the source of infinite supply.

The Soul-conscious people of this world live an inner life of peace, joy and dominion and an outer life in complete harmony with itself and with all the world of men, animals and things. They are in tune with their

Soul-powers and this constitutes their at-one-ment with all creation.

3   Every one may have access to the Soul. It lies deep within the recesses of our own be-ing. Desire for the higher attainments of life

6   is the first requisite; and then a continuous turning within until the goal has been at-tained.

9   A good start may be made through the realization of the truth that there is more to even human existence than corporeal

12 health and material supply. When we catch a glimpse of the fact that more dollars, homes or automobiles do not constitute sup-

15 ply; that more travel does not constitute rec-reation; that absence of illness is not neces-sarily health; in other words, that "My king-

18 dom is not of this world," we are going in the right direction to discover the realm of Soul.

21   We all know how to use material force as when we lift some weight through the strength of our muscles, or exert pressure

24 through arms or legs, and we also under-stand how to exert mental pressure as in deep thought or through personal will.

SOUL

That there is a Soul-force we know, and
that this Soul-power can do more for us
than all the material and mental power com- 3
bined is but little suspected. Perhaps one
reason for the world's lack of interest in
this vast subject is that this great reservoir 6
of power resident in our Soul cannot be used
for selfish purposes. Think of the enormity
of this — a great marvelous power at hand 9
and yet it can never be used to serve a selfish
end. Herein lies the secret of why so few
achieve Soul consciousness. We only be- 12
come aware of the presence of the Soul after
we have freed ourselves of selfish desires
and in proportion to our desire to serve the 15
interests of mankind do we individualize
this infinite power within us. It is right,
natural and normal that we live full, happy 18
and prosperous lives but we can do this
without taking thought for ourselves, for
our supply, or even our health. All of the 21
good necessary to our welfare will be supplied to us in greater abundance than we
could accept when we give up the effort and 24
desire to get, achieve or accomplish, and
come more into the consciousness of desir-

ing only to fulfill our destiny on earth. We are here as part of a divine plan. We are

3 Mind fulfilling and expressing itself in an individual way, and if we will learn to keep our thought away from ourselves and away

6 from the fear that we will be without place or income or health, and let Mind fulfill its destiny through us or as us, we will really

9 find all things added unto us. The Bible is literally true when it says that "the earth is the Lord's and the fulness thereof" and

12 "Son, . . . all that I have is thine." There is no need therefore to take any anxious thought for our own well-being. As we for-

15 get ourselves and learn to be a state of receptivity we will find ourselves filled with Soul power, Soul consciousness, Soul re-

18 sources, and our lives will be filled with the company of Soul-filled men and women sharing the joys of their discoveries with us.

21 The Mind that was in Christ Jesus is not afar off; nor is it the Mind of only a few great religious leaders; the Mind that was

24 in Christ Jesus is your Mind and it is ready to impart itself to you as you forget self and become receptive to the divine wisdom with-

in you. The resources of Soul are waiting at the door of your consciousness ready to pour forth more than you can accept, but 3 not to satisfy some personal or selfish desire. These false desires are the stumbling blocks to our spiritual development and we 6 must not think to use our spiritual powers to gain personal and selfish ends. The song of the Soul is freedom, joy and eternal bliss; 9 the song of the Soul is love to all mankind; the song of the Soul is you.

Why are we so slow in gaining our free- 12 dom from illness, discord and other material conditions? It is entirely because of our inability to grasp the great revelation that 15 there is no reality to error.

So much attention has been given to faith in God to do something for us; or to faith 18 in a healer or teacher, that we have overlooked the great truth — error is not real — there is no matter. 21

We are learning from physical scientists as well as metaphysicians that what has been termed matter is a misinterpretation of 24 Mind. Mind is God and God is Spirit, therefore all that exists is spiritual substance regardless of the name or nature ascribed to it by finite sense.

3 God is the Mind of the individual, therefore all that can come to us as person, thing or condition is coming to us as Mind, in 6 Mind and through Mind, and God, Mind, is the Soul of every individual; God, Principle, is the law of all action; God, Spirit, is the 9 substance of all of which we are conscious.

Through false education, which constitutes finite sense, we have come to fear certain 12 individuals, things and conditions, not realizing that as these are coming to us through the avenue of consciousness they 15 are all God-being, Mind-appearing, Spirit-substance. Material consciousness is the false finite sense which beholds the universe and 18 man as limited; as being both good and evil. Spiritual consciousness is the awareness of the individual as God-being; as having only 21 the Mind which is God and the body of Spirit. It recognizes the entire universe as Mind-appearing and governed by divine 24 Principle. Spiritual consciousness is the ability to see beyond the appearance to Reality. It is the recognition and realization that as God is our Mind, all that appears to us is in and of God which is our only consciousness.　　3

Spiritual consciousness does not overcome or destroy matter or material conditions but knows that no such conditions exist which　6 finite sense presents. It translates the appearance for us, revealing the true nature of that which is appearing.　　9

Spiritual power emanates from the Soul — the Soul of you and the Soul of me. It is impersonal and impartial. Everyone may　12 open the windows of his Soul and behold the infinite glories of a world far above the universe of sense. Far greater than anything　15 we have ever seen or heard is the world of the Soul, the world that is seen through spiritual sense. We know that unillumined　18 thought beholds the universe as material, whereas the illumined consciousness, or Soul-sense, sees and undestands the universe　21 as spiritual.

There is nothing impractical about the development of our spiritual sense or Soul　24 powers. This uplifted consciousness enabled Moses to lead his people out of bondage and through the Red Sea into the awareness of abundance. Through Jesus it healed the multitudes of their diseases, fed the multitudes with actual food, and raised the dead. Through Paul it lifted a portion of humanity above the deepest sorrows and persecutions into Christ Consciousness and spiritual freedom.

Spiritual consciousness lifts us above every human form of limitation and permits us to enter a larger sense of life, health and freedom. Where there is spiritual consciousness there is no bondage to person, place nor thing and there are no limitations to our accomplishments.

So far as is known, Jesus never left a written word, and yet his teaching is the foundation of the morals and ethics for much of the world. Many other seers left only the Word spoken to their immediate followers, yet by their own power these messages have become living Waters through countless ages. The wisdom of the ages, uttered by spiritually illumined men and women who never dreamed that their thoughts would circle the globe and influ-

ence the lives and conduct of people, is not
confined to time or place. The Christ-like
thoughts that fill their consciousness go out 3
from them like the ring created by throwing
a stone in the water, making an ever-widen-
ing circle until it embraces all humanity. 6
Yes, spiritual consciousness is practical. Our
desire for affluence must be the desire for
the other fellow's affluence before we can 9
experience the grace which is the gift of
God.

Meditation is the door to the realm of 12
the Soul and inspiration is the Way. As we
learn to take five or ten minutes each morning, noon and night to sit quietly with 15
"listening" ear; as we turn within ourselves
and learn to wait for the "still small voice,"
we acquire the habit of meditation and de- 18
velop skill in its technique until inspiration
possesses us and leads us to the haven of our
Soul. This is the beginning of our new birth 21
and here we learn the new tongue of Spirit.
Life begins to have a new meaning.

MEDITATION

To MEDITATE IS "to fix the mind upon; think about continuously; contemplate; to engage in continuous and contemplated thought; dwell mentally on anything; ruminate and cogitate."

In the spiritual tongue meditation is prayer. True prayer or meditation is not a thinking about ourselves or our problems but rather the contemplation of God and God activities, and the nature of God, and the nature of the world that God created.

Everyone should take some time daily to retire to a quiet spot for meditation. During this period he should turn his thought to God, and consider his understanding of God, and search out a deeper understanding of the nature of Spirit and its formations, and of Mind and its infinite manifestation. He should be careful not to take any of his ills or other problems into his meditation. This particular period is set

aside, dedicated and consecrated to thinking
about God and God's universe.

As God is the Mind and Soul of every 3
individual, it is possible for all of us to be
tuned in to the kingdom of God and receive
the divine messages and assurances and 6
benefits of the one infinite Love. The grace
of God which we receive in these periods
of meditation or prayer becomes tangible 9
to us in the fulfilling of our so-called human needs. If we do not open our consciousness to the reception of spiritual understand- 12
ing we must not be surprised if we do not
experience spiritual good in our daily living, and there is no other way to open our 15
consciousness to the realm of Soul than
through meditation or prayer, through con-
templating the things of God. "Thou wilt 18
keep him in perfect peace whose mind is
stayed on Thee."

All through the day our thoughts are 21
centered on the activities of human experience, on family cares and duties and earning
a livelihood, on social and community af- 24
fairs, and sometimes even on greater affairs of state. Is it not natural then that at

some time during the day or evening we take time off to retire to our inner conscious-
3 ness, which is the Temple of God, and there dwell upon the things of God. Above all we must develop the sense of receptivity so
6 that we can become ever more aware of the very presence of God in His Holy Temple which is our consciousness. In the secret
9 place of the Most High, which is the Holy of Holies, which is our very own inner con-sciousness, we receive illumination, guid-
12 ance, wisdom and spiritual power. "In quiet-ness and confidence shall be my strength."

As we learn to listen to the "still small
15 voice" the Spirit of God opens our conscious-ness to the immediate awareness of spiritual good. We are filled with the divine ener-
18 gies of Spirit; we are illumined with the light of the Soul; we are refreshed with the waters of Life and fed with the meat which
21 does not perish. This spiritual food is never rationed to those who learn to meet God within the temple of their being.
24 To receive the grace of God we must re-tire from the world of sense, we must learn to silence the material senses and have au-

dience with God. God must become to us a living reality, a divine presence, a Holy Spirit within, and this can only be when we 3 have learned to meditate, pray, contemplate God.

Through meditation we become aware of 6 the presence of the Christ and this awareness remains with us all day and all night as we go about our human existence. This 9 awareness enters into our every experience and prospers every endeavor. This consciousness of the presence of Christ is a light 12 unto our feet and a guiding star unto our aspirations. It is the presence that goes before us to make the crooked places straight. 15 It is the quality in our consciousness that makes us understood and appreciated by others. 18

On awaking in the morning, and preferably before you get out of bed, turn your thought to the realization that "I and my 21 Father are one"; that "Son. . . . all that I have is thine"; that "The place whereon thou standest is holy ground"; then let the mean- 24 ing of these statements unfold from within your own consciousness. Gain a conviction of your oneness with the Father, with the universal Life, the universal Mind, the universal Consciousness. Feel the infinity of good within you which is the evidence of your oneness with the infinite source of your being.

As soon as you begin to feel a stirring within you, or a sense of peace, or the surge of divine Life, then get out of bed and make your physical preparations for the day. Before leaving your home sit down and ponder your oneness with God.

The wave is one with the ocean, indivisible and inseparable from the whole ocean. All that the ocean is the wave is, and all the power, all the energy, all the strength, all the life, all the substance of the ocean is expressed in every wave. The wave has access to all that lies beneath it for the wave really is the ocean as the ocean is the wave, inseparable, indivisible, one. And note here this very important point, that there is no place where one wave comes to an end and the next wave begins, so that the oneness of the wave with the ocean includes the oneness of every wave with every other wave.

MEDITATION

As a wave is one with the ocean, so you are one with God. Your oneness with the universal Life constitues your oneness with every individual expression of that Life; your oneness with divine Mind constitutes your oneness with every idea of Mind. As the infinity of God surges through you to bless all with whom you come in contact, remember that the infinity of God is also surging through every other individual on earth to you. No one is sharing anything with you that is of themselves, but all that they have is of the Father, so everything that you have is of the Father and you are sharing it with all the world. You are one with the Father, with the universal Consciousness, and you are one with every spiritual idea of which this Consciousness is conscious.

This is a tremendous idea if you get it. It means that your interest is the interest of every individual in the world; it means that their interest is your interest; it means that we have no interest apart from each other even as we have no interest apart from God; it means actually that all that the Father hath is ours and all that we have is for the benefit of everyone else as everything that they have is for our benefit, and all for the

3 glory of God.

Now this idea must unfold within you in an original way. It must, bit by bit and day

6 by day, unfold in different ways, and always with greater meaning because of the infinity of Mind's ideas. You might note

9 how a tree has many branches and how all of these branches are at one with the trunk of the tree and therefore with the root of

12 the tree, and that the root of the tree is one with the earth and is drawing into it all that the earth possesses. And further, that each

15 branch is not only one with the whole tree but each branch is one with every branch, connected parts of one whole. As you pon-

18 der this idea of your oneness with God and your oneness with every individual spiritual idea, new ideas along this line will unfold

21 to you, new illustrations, original illustrations and symbols. By the time you have concluded this morning meditation you will

24 find that you will actually feel the presence of God within you; you will actually feel the divine energy of Spirit; you will feel the

surge of new life within you, and this too
will lead on to other thoughts.

Whenever you leave one place to go to 3
another place, such as leaving your home for
business, or leaving your business for church,
or going back to your home, pause for a 6
second to realize that the Presence has gone
before you to prepare the way, and that that
same divine Presence remains behind you as 9
a benediction to all who pass that way. At
first you may forget to do this many times
during the day but by jogging your memory 12
you will eventually find that this will become an established activity of your consciousness and you will never make a move 15
without realizing the divine Presence ahead
of you and behind you, and in this way you
will find yourself to be the Light of the 18
world.

One of the subjects near and dear to us
these past few years is that of peace, and 21
we can have no faith in any perpetual peace
based on whatever human documents or
organizations can be formulated. True, they 24
have their purpose and they are a necessary
step for humans just as the Ten Command-

ments were a necessary step until the
Sermon on the Mount replaced them with
3 higher vision. You do not need the Ten
Commandments because you need no admo-
nition not to steal or lie or cheat, nor do you
6 need any threat of punishment to keep you
honest, clean and pure, but the Ten Commandments are necessary to those who have
9 not yet learned righteousness for righteousness' sake. In the same way the world is
greatly in need of some kind of a human
12 organization and some kind of human document to keep some form or some measure of
peace in the world. But the real peace, the
15 lasting peace, will only come as it has come
to you individually through the realization
that you do not need anything that the other
18 fellow has and therefore there is nothing to
war about. All that the Father hath is yours,
what can you want beside that? As a matter
21 of fact, as joint heir with Christ in God you
could feed five thousand any day and every
day without ever taking thought as to
24 whence it should come.

When all mankind comes into this consciousness of its true identity there will be

no wars, no competition, no strife. As you
gain the full consciousness of your true
identity you show it forth in a greater sense 3
of harmony, health and success, and one by
one you attract others who are seeking the
same way. In this way all men will ulti- 6
mately be brought into the kingdom of
heaven.

PRAYER

"Y E ASK, and receive not, because ye ask amiss," says the Apostle James. Have you ever thought of this when you have prayed for some time, and then found no answer to your prayer? "Ye ask amiss." There is the reason.

Prayer, when based on the belief that there is a need unfilled, a desire unsatisfied, is never in accord with true scientific prayer. A prayer for God to do something, send something, provide or heal, is equally without power.

It is sometimes believed that God requires a channel through which to fulfill our prayer; and this leads us to look outside ourselves for the answer. We may believe that supply can come to us, and therefore we watch for the person or position through which it is to come. We may be depending on a healer or teacher as the channel through which the healing is to come. "Ye ask amiss."

Any belief that that which we are seeking 3 is anywhere but within *us,* within our very own consciousness, is the barrier, separating us in belief from our harmony. 6

True prayer is never addressed to a Being outside ourselves, nor does true prayer expect anything from outside our own be- 9 ing. "The kingdom of God is within you" and all good must be sought there. Recognizing God to be the reality of our being, 12 we know that all good is inherent in that Being, your being and mine. God is the substance of our being and therefore we are 15 eternal and harmonious. God is Life, and this Life is self-sustained. He is our Soul, and we are pure and immortal. God is the 18 Mind of the individual and this constitutes the intelligence of our being.

Rightly speaking, there is not God and 21 you, but God is ever manifest *as* you and this is the oneness which assures you of infinite good. God is the Life, Mind, Body and 24 Substance of individual being, therefore nothing can be added to any individual, and true prayer is the constant recognition of this truth.

3 Conscious awareness of our true being — of the infinite nature and character of our only being — this, too, is prayer. In this

6 consciousness, instead of seeking, asking, waiting, in prayer, we turn our thought inward and listen for the "still small voice"

9 which assures us that even before we asked our Father knew and fulfilled the need. Here is the great secret of prayer, that God

12 is All-in-all and God is forever manifested. There is no unmanifested good or God. That which we seem to be seeking is ever-

15 present within us, and already manifested, and we need to know this truth. All good already is, and is forever manifested. *The*

18 *recognition of this truth is answered prayer.* Our health, wealth, employment, home, harmony, etc., are then not dependent on

21 some far-off God; are never dependent on a channel or person or place, but are eternally at hand, omnipresent, within our very

24 consciousness, and the recognition of this fact is answered prayer. "I and my Father

are one," and this accounts for the completeness of individual being.

Properly speaking, there is not God and 3
you. It is impossible to pray aright unless
this truth is understood. Prayer becomes
but blind faith or belief rather than under- 6
standing, when we do not know our real
relationship with Deity. It is our conscious
awareness of the oneness of Being — the 9
oneness of Life, Mind, Truth, Love — that
results in answered prayer. It is the constant
recognition of our life, our mind, our sub- 12
stance and activity as the manifestation of
God-being that constitutes true prayer. As
we identify this God-being as the only reality 15
of our individual being, we are able to
comprehend ourselves as the fulfillment of
God; as the completeness and the perfec- 18
tion of being, all inclusive, immortal and
divine. The recognition of the divinity of
our individual being embracing and in- 21
cluding the allness of God, is true prayer
which is ever-answered prayer. The correc-
tion of the belief that we are ever separate 24
or apart from our good, is the essence of
true prayer. *That which I am seeking, I am.*

107

Whatever it is of good that I have believed to be separate from me is, in fact, a con-
3 stituted part of my being. I include, embody and embrace within myself, within my consciousness, the reality of God which forms
6 the infinity of health, wealth and harmony of my being. The conscious awareness of this truth is true prayer.

9 Despite the Allness of God expressed as perfect individual being, there constantly arises in human experience those ills which
12 call forth our understanding of prayer. What is the nature of error, sin, disease? How can such things be *and God be All-in-*
15 *all?* Such things cannot be and are not, despite the appearance of pain and discord and sorrow.

18 The Bible reveals to us the basic truth of being, namely, that "God saw every thing that He had made, and, behold, it was very
21 good." In this All-good that God made, there is nothing that "defileth . . . or maketh a lie." And there is no other creative Prin-
24 ciple. It becomes clear then that that which is appearing as error, sin, disease, pain and discord, is illusion, mirage, nothingness.

PRAYER

Let us then, as part of our prayer, remember that God made (evolved) all that was made, and in this universe of God there is 3 only the All-Presence and All-Power of God, divine Love, and that therefore that which at the moment appears to us as error 6 is a false sense of Reality.

There comes a time in our experience when spiritual inspiration reveals to individ- 9 ual consciousness a state of being free of mortal conditions and beliefs. Then we no longer live a life of mental affirmations and 12 denials, but rather receive constant unfoldments of Truth from Mind. Sometimes this comes through no other channel than our 15 own thought. It may come through a book or lecture or a service imparted by divine Consciousness. Regardless of the seeming 18 channel through which it may come, it is Mind revealing itself to individual consciousness. 21

As we become more and more consciously aware of our oneness with the universal or Christ Mind, whatever desires or 24 needs come to us, bring with them their fulfillment of every righteous thought and

wish. Is it not clear then that our oneness
with Mind being established "in the begin-
3 ning" through the relationship forever existing between God and His manifested being,
it requires no conscious effort to bring about
6 or maintain. The awareness of this truth is
the connecting link with divine Consciousness.

9 To many prayer means supplication and
petition to a God in a place called heaven.
That this prayer has resulted so universally
12 in failure to attain its ends must prove that
this is not prayer and that the God prayed
to is not there listening. Human thought
15 eventually realized the lack of answer to
such prayers and turned to a search for the
true God and the right concept of prayer.
18 This led to a revelation of Truth as understood and practiced by Christ Jesus and
many earlier revelators.

21 Here we learn that "the kingdom of God
is within you" and therefore prayer must
be directed within to that point in conscious-
24 ness where the universal Life, God, becomes
individualized as you or as me. We learn
that God created (evolved) the world in

the beginning and that "it was good." Being good, the universe must inevitably be complete, harmonious and perfect so that 3 instead of pleading for good, our prayer becomes the realization of the omnipresence of good, and so the higher concept reveals 6 prayer as the affirmation of good and the denial of the existence of error as Reality.

When the prayer of affirmation results in 9 the use of formulas it has a tendency to revert to old-fashioned faith-prayer and thereby loses potency. When, however, one's 12 prayer consists of spontaneous and sincere affirmations of the infinity of God and of the harmony and perfection of His manifes- 15 tation, one is indeed nearing the absolute of prayer, which is communion with God.

Before our enlightenment in Truth we 18 prayed for things and persons. We sought to gain some personal end. With his great vision Emerson wrote: "Prayer that craves 21 a particular commodity, anything less than all good, is vicious." Then this wise man defines prayer for us: "Prayer is the con- 24 templation of the facts of life from the highest point of view. It is the soliloquy of

111

a beholding and jubilant soul. It is the spirit
of God pronouncing His works good . . .
3 As soon as the man is one with God, he will
not beg." Prayer must not be understood as
going to God for something for, as Emer-
6 son continues, "Prayer as a means to effect
a private end is meanness and theft."

Well, now we know what prayer is not,
9 and have glimpsed that prayer is the union
of our self, the individual Soul, with God,
the universal Soul. Actually the individual
12 Soul and the universal Soul are not two,
but one, but the conscious awareness of this
truth constitutes the union or oneness which
15 is true prayer.

Jesus said, "My kingdom is not of this
world," and this we must remember when
18 we pray. To go to God carrying some recol-
lection, some demand, some desire of this
world, must end fruitlessly. When we enter
21 our sanctuary of Spirit, we must leave outside all wordly wishes, needs, and lacks. We
must drop "this world" and go to God with
24 but one idea — communion with God,
union or oneness with God. We must not
pray to gain, to have changed or corrected.

PRAYER

Prayer which is conscious oneness with God always results in bringing forth harmony, peace, joy, success. These are the "added things." It is not that Spirit produces or heals or corrects matter or the physical universe, but that we rise higher in consciousness to where there is less matter and therefore less discord, inharmony, disease or lack.

Communion with God is true prayer. It is the unfoldment in individual consciousness of His Presence and Power, and it makes you "every whit whole." Communion with God is in reality listening for the "still small voice." In this communion, or prayer, no words pass from you to God, but the consciousness of the presence of God is realized as the impartation of Truth and Love comes from God within, to you. It is a holy state of being and never leaves us where it finds us.

METAPHYSICAL HEALING

HEALINGS ARE always in proportion to our understanding of the truth about God, man, idea, body. Healing has nothing to do with someone "out there" called a patient. When anyone asks for spiritual help or healing, that ends their part in what follows until they acknowledge their so-called healing. We are not concerned with the so-called patient, the claim, the cause of the illness or its nature, nor with his sins or fears. We are now concerned only with the truth of being — the truth of God, man, idea, body. The activity of this truth in our consciousness is the Christ, Saviour or healing influence.

Failure to heal is the result of much mis-knowledge of the truth of God, man, idea, body, and this mis-knowledge stems primarily from orthodox religious beliefs which have not been rooted out of our thought.

Few realize to what extent they are blinded by superstitious orthodoxy.

There is only one answer to the question, 3 What is God? and that answer is I AM. God is the Mind, the Life of the individual. Any mental hedging or inner reservation on 6 this subject will result in ultimate failure. There is but one universal I whether it is being spoken by Jesus Christ or John Smith. 9 When Jesus revealed: "He that seeth me seeth him that sent me," he was revealing a universal Truth or Principle. There must be 12 no quibbling about this. You either understand this truth or you do not — and if you do not there is no need for you to seek any 15 further reason for failure to heal. The revelation of Jesus the Christ is clear. "I am the way, the truth, and the life." Unless you can 18 accept this as a principle, therefore as the truth about you and about every individual, you have no foundation upon which to stand. 21 The truth is that God is the Mind and Life of the individual. God is the only "I."

Next comes the question, What is man? 24 and the answer is that man is idea, body, manifestation. My body is idea, or manifes-

tation. Likewise my business, home, wealth,
— these exist as idea or manifestation, ex-
3 pression, reflection. For this reason and for
no other my body is the exact image and
likeness of my consciousness and reflects
6 or expresses the qualities, character and nature of my own consciousness of existence.

So far then we understand that "I" am
9 God; that God is the Mind and Life of the
individual; that my body exists as the idea
of God. God, or I AM, is universal, infinite,
12 omnipotent and omnipresent; therefore, the
idea body is equally indestructible, im-
perishable, eternal. It was never born and
15 will never die. I shall never be without the
conscious awareness of my body; therefore,
I shall never be without my body.

18 When we look out upon the world with
our eyes we are not beholding our bodies,
we are not seeing this infinite divine idea
21 body, we are beholding a more or less universal *concept* of the idea. As we see a
healthy body, a beautiful flower or tree, we
24 are seeing a good concept of the idea body,
flower, tree. When we see an aging, ailing
body or withered flower or decaying tree, we

are beholding an erroneous concept of the divine idea. As we improve our concepts of idea, body, manifestation, we term this improving of concepts, *healing*. Actually nothing has happened to the so-called patient or his body — the change has come in the individual's consciousness and becomes visible as improved belief or healing. For this reason the healer alone must accept responsibility for healing and never try to shift the blame for non-healing onto the person who asked for help. *That individual is I AM, Life, Truth and Love, and his body exists as perfect spiritual eternal harmonious idea subject only to the laws of Principle, Mind, Soul, Spirit* — and it is our privilege, duty and responsibility to know this truth and the truth will make free every person who turns to us.

As individual, infinite spiritual consciousness, I embody my universe, I embody or include the idea body, home, activity, income, health, wealth, companionship, and these are subject only to spiritual law and life. The body is not self-acting, it is governed harmoniously by spiritual power. When the

body appears to be discordant, inactive,
overactive, changing, paining, it is always
3 the belief that the body is self-acting; that
it of itself has the power to move or not
move, to ache, pain, sicken or die. This is
6 not true. The body is not self-acting. It has
no intelligence or activity of its own. All
action is Mind action, therefore omnipotent
9 good action. When we know this truth, the
body responds to this knowing or understanding of Truth. No change then takes
12 place in the body because the error never
was there. It is entirely exchanging a concept for the truth that already is, always
15 has been and ever will be. Remember there
is no patient "out there" and no body out
there to be healed, improved or corrected.
18 Always it is a false concept or belief to be
corrected in individual thought.

When we begin to understand that the
21 body is not self-acting; that it responds only
to the stimulus of Mind, we can disregard
so-called inharmonious bodily conditions and
24 abide in the truth that Life is forever expressing itself harmoniously, perfectly and
eternally as the divine idea, body.

The understanding that I AM—individual infinite spiritual consciousness embodying every right idea and governing them har- 3 moniously — brings forth health, harmony, home, employment, recognition, peace, joy and dominion. The understanding that this 6 is true of every individual dispels the illusion of hate, enmity, opposition, etc. This also makes of you a practitioner, a healer, a 9 teacher, whether or not professionally engaged in the work.

We come now to face our orthodox 12 superstitions and to leave them. Was Jesus sent into the world by God to save it from sin, disease, or slavery? No. God, the in- 15 finite Principle, Life, Truth and Love, knows no error, no evil, no sin and no sinner. Jesus so clearly apprehended this truth 18 that this apprehension became the Saviour, Healer, Teacher even as it will in you. *The activity of Truth in individual consciousness* 21 *is the only Christ.* No person is ever the Christ. The activity of Truth in individual consciousness constitutes the only Christ, 24 the ever-present Christ who was "before Abraham." The activity of Truth in your

consciousness is the Christ of you. The activity of Truth in the consciousness of
3 Buddha revealed the nature of sin, disease and death to be illusion or mirage. The activity of Truth in the consciousness of
6 Jesus Christ revealed the nothingness of matter; it unfolded as a Healing Consciousness before which sin and disease disap-
9 peared and death was overcome. Every erroneous concept, whether of body or business, health or church, must disappear as
12 the right idea of these appear in individual and collective consciousness.

What about immaculate conception or
15 spiritual birth? The immaculate conception or spiritual birth is the dawning in individual consciousness of the activity of Truth
18 or Christ idea. It appeared in Jesus as the revelation that "I am the way, the truth, and the life" "I am the resurrection and the
21 life"—"He that seeth me, seeth him that sent me." The activity of Truth in my consciousness, the Christ of me, is revealing
24 that I am individual, infinite, spiritual consciousness embodying my universe, including my body, my health, wealth, practice, in-

come, home, companionship, eternality and immortality.

Let the activity of Truth in your consciousness be your first and last and only concern, and the Christ of you will also reveal itself in an individual, infinite Way.

There is no evil. Let us therefore stop the resistance to the particular discord or inharmony of human existence which now confronts us. These apparent discords will disappear as we are able to cease our resistance to them. We are able to do this only in proportion to our realization of the spiritual nature of the universe. Since this is true, it is evident that neither heaven nor earth can contain error of any nature and therefore the unillumined human thought is seeing error in the very place where God shines through; discord where harmony is; hate where love abounds; fear where confidence really is.

The work on which we have embarked is the realization that we are individual infinite spiritual consciousness embodying within ourselves all good. This is the song we will sing, the sermon we will preach, the lesson we will teach, and until realization comes, this is our theme, our motif. It is the silver cord of Truth running through every message.

Nothing can come to you; nothing can be added. You are already that place in consciousness through which infinity is pouring. That which we term your humanhood must be still so as to be a clear transparency through which your infinite individual Self may appear, express or reveal itself.

When we view Niagara Falls from the front, we might assume that it could run dry with so much water continually pouring over the Falls. Looking behind the immediate scene, we behold Lake Erie, and realize that actually there is no Niagara, that this is but a name given to Lake Erie at a point where Erie pours over the Falls. The infinity of Niagara Falls is assured by virtue of the fact that actually the source of Niagara, that which constitutes Niagara, is really Lake Erie.

So with us. We are that place where God becomes visible. We are the Word made flesh. Our source, and that which constitutes us, is God—infinite divine Being. We are God-being, God-appearing, God-manifesting. That is the true glory of our being. 3

The story is told of Marconi, that when he was very young, he told friends that he 6 would be the one to give wireless to the world and not the many older seekers who had been experimenting for years. After 9 he fulfilled his promise he was asked why he had been so certain that he would succeed. His answer was that the other sci- 12 entists were seeking first to discover a means to overcome resistance in the air to the messages that would be sent through the 15 air, whereas he had already discovered there was no resistance.

The world is fighting a power of evil; we 18 have discovered there is no such power. While materia medica seeks to overcome or cure disease and theology struggles to 21 overcome sin, we have learned there is no reality to disease or sin and our so-called healings are brought about through this 24 understanding.

We know that there are these human

appearances called sin and disease, but we know that because of the infinite spiritual
3 nature of our being, they are not realities of being; they are not evil power; they have no Principle to support them; there-
6 fore, they exist only as unrealities accepted as realities, illusion accepted as condition, the misinterpretation of what actually is.
9 We bind ourselves by believing there is power outside of us—power for good or for evil. All power is given to *you*. And this
12 power is always good because of the infinite source whence it flows. The recognition of this great fact brings a peace and a
15 joy untold, yet felt by all who come within range of your thought. It makes you beloved of men. It brings you recognition and
18 reward. It establishes you in the thoughts of men and becomes the foundation of an eternal good will.
21 Whenever you are faced with a problem, regardless of its nature, seek the solution within your own consciousness. Instead of
24 running around here and there; instead of seeking an answer from this or that person; instead of looking for the solution outside

of yourself, turn within. In the quiet and calm of your own mind, let the answer to your problem unfold itself. If, the first or 3 second or third time you turn in peace to the kingdom within, you fail to perceive the completed picture, try again. You will not 6 be too late, nor will the solution appear too late. As you learn to depend on this means for the working out of your problems and 9 experiences, you will become more and more adept in quickly discerning your mind's revelation of harmony. Too long have we 12 sought our health, peace and prosperity outside ourselves. Now let us go within and learn that there is never a failure nor a dis- 15 appointment in the whole realm of our consciousness. Nor will we ever find delays or betrayals when we find the calm of our 18 own Soul and the presence of an infinite Principle governing, guarding, guiding and protecting every step of our journey through 21 life.

Do not be surprised now when the outstanding truth unfolds to you that your 24 consciousness is the all-power and the only power acting upon your affairs, controlling and maintaining your health, revealing to you the intelligence and direction necessary for your success in any and every walk of life. Does this astonish you? No wonder! Heretofore you have believed that somewhere there existed a deific power, a supreme presence, which, *if you could reach,* might aid you or even heal your body of its ills. Now it becomes clear to you that the universal Mind or Consciousness is the mind of the individual man and *it* is the all-power and ever-presence which can never leave you nor forsake you, and it is "closer than breathing." And you need not pray to it, petition it or in any way seek its favor,—you need but this recognition leading to the complete realization of this truth. From now on you will relax and *feel* the constant assurance of the presence and power of this illumined consciousness. You can now say, "I will not fear what man shall do unto me." No more will you fear conditions or circumstances seemingly outside of you or beyond your control. Now you know that all that can transpire in your experience is occurring within your consciousness and therefore subject to its government and control.

Nor will you ever forget the depth of 3 feeling accompanying this revelation within you, nor the sense of confidence and courage that immediately follows it. Life is no longer 6 a problem-filled series of events, but a joyous succession of unfolding delights. Failure is recognized as the result of a uni- 9 versal belief in a power outside of ourselves. Success is the natural consequence of our realization of infinite power within. 12

Release from fear, worry and doubt leaves us free to function normally, healthfully and confidently. The body acts immediately from 15 the stimulus coming to it from within. New vitality, strength and bodily peace follow as naturally as rest follows sleep. Little do 18 we know of the depth of the riches within us until we come to know the realm of our own consciousness, the kingdom of our 21 mind.

When we become still and go into the temple of our being for the answer to some 24 important question, or the solution of a vital problem, it is well that we do not formulate some idea of our own, or outline a plan, or let our wish in the matter father our thought. Rather should we still the thinking mind so far as possible and adopt a listening attitude. It is not the personal sense of mind (or conscious mind) which is to supply the answer. Nor is it the educated mind or the mind formed of our environment and experience, but the universal Mind, the Reality of us, the creative Consciousness. And this is best heard when the senses and reasoning mind are silent.

This inner Mind not only shows us the solution to any problem and the right direction to take in any situation, but, being the universal Mind, it is the consciousness of every individual and brings every person and circumstance together for the good of the whole.

Obviously we cannot look to this universal Consciousness to work with us for anyone's destruction or loss. What is accomplished in and through the kingdom of our mind is always constructive individually and collectively. It can therefore never be the means of harm, loss or injury to another.

Nor do we direct our thought at another, or project it outside ourselves in any direction. That which our mind is unfolding to us, is at the time operating as the consciousness of all concerned. We need never concern ourselves with "reaching" some other mind, or influencing some other person. Remember that the activity of Mind unfolding as us, is the influence unto all who can possibly be affected by or concerned in the problem or situation. There are no unsolved problems in Mind and this same Mind which is our own consciousness is the only power necessary to establishing and maintaining the harmony of all that concerns us. It is our turning within that brings forth the answer already established. Our listening attitude makes us receptive to the presence and the power within us. Our periods of silent contemplation reveal the infinite force and constructive energy and intelligent direction always abiding in us. Thus we discover in our mental realm the Aladdin's Lamp. Instead of rubbing and wishing, we turn in silence and listen—and all that is necessary for the harmony and success of life flows

forth abundantly and we learn to live joyously, healthfully, and successfully—not by
reason of any person or circumstance outside ourselves, but because of the influence
and grace within our own being.

No longer is it necessary to try to dominate our business associates or members of
our family. The law within us maintains
our rights and privileges. Every right desire
of our heart is fulfilled now and without
struggle or strife, without fear or doubt.
The more we learn to relax and quickly contemplate our real desires, the more quickly
and more easily are they achieved. It is not
required of us that we suffer our way
through life or strive endlessly for some
desired good—but we have failed to perceive the presence of an inner law capable
of establishing and maintaining our outer
welfare.

It seems strange to us at first to realize
that inner laws govern outer events—and it
may at first appear difficult to achieve the
state of consciousness wherein these laws of
our inner being come into tangible expression. We will achieve it, however, in pro-

portion to our ability to relax mentally; to gain an inner calm and peace; and therein quietly contemplate the revelations which come to us from within. Quietness and confidence soon bring us face to face with Reality, the real laws governing us.

Lest the question should arise in your thought as to how a law operating in your consciousness (and without conscious effort or direction) can affect individuals and circumstances outside yourself, let me ask you to watch the result of your recognition of the inner laws and learn this through observation.

We are yet to become aware of the fact that we embrace our world within ourselves; that all that exists as persons, places and things lives only within our own consciousness. We could never become aware of anything outside the realm of our own mind. And all that is within our mental kingdom is joyously and harmoniously directed and sustained by the laws within. We do not direct or enforce these laws; they eternally operate within us and govern the world without.

The peace within becomes the harmony without. As our thought takes on the nature of the inner freedom, it loses its sense of fear, doubt, or discouragement. As the realization of our dominion dawns in thought, more assurance, confidence and certainty become evident. We become a new being, and the world reflects back to us our own higher attitude toward it. Gradually an understanding of our fellow man and his problems unfolds to us from within, and more love flows out from us, more tolerance, co-operativeness, helpfulness, and compassion, and we find the world responds to our newer concept of it, and then all the universe rushes to us to pour its riches and treasures in our lap.

Many fine treaties and covenants have been signed by nations and men, and nearly all have failed, because no document is any better than the character of those who administer it. When we become imbued with the fire of our inner being, we no longer need contracts and agreements in writing because it becomes first nature with us to be just, honest, intelligent and kind—and these qualities are met in all those who become part of our experience in the home, office, shop, and in all our walks of life. 3 The good revealed in our consciousness returns to us, "pressed down, shaken together, and running over." 6

In this new consciousness we are less angered by the acts of other people; less impatient with their short-comings; less disturbed by their failings. And likewise, instead of being hampered and restricted by external conditions, we either do not meet with them 12 or else brush right by them with but little concern. We realize that something within us is ruling our universe; an inner presence 15 is maintaining outer harmony. The peace and quiet of our own Soul is the law of harmony and success to our world of daily 18 experience.

All that has gone before this is as nothing unless you have seen that over and above 21 all "knowing the truth," you must be overshadowed by the Christ.

When the Christ dawns in individual con- 24 sciousness, the sense of personal self diminishes. This Christ becomes our real being.

We have no desires, no will, no power of our own. The Christ overshadows our personal selfhood. We still perceive in the background this finite sense and at times it tries to assert itself and even dominate the scene. "For the good that I would I do not: but the evil which I would not, that I do," says Paul.

But let it be clear to you that the personal self cannot heal, teach or govern harmoniously. It must be held in abeyance that the Christ may have full dominion within our consciousness.

The work that is done with the letter of Truth, with declarations and so-called treatments, is insignificant compared with what is accomplished when we have surrendered our will and action to the Christ.

Christ comes to our consciousness most clearly in those moments when we come face to face with problems for which we have no answer, and no power to surmount, and we realize that "I can of mine own self do nothing." In these moments of self-effacement, the gentle Christ overshadows us, permeates our consciousness and brings the "Peace, be still," to the troubled mind.

In this Christ we find rest, peace, comfort and healing. The unlabored power of 3 spiritual sense possesses us and discords and inharmonies fade away as darkness disappears with the coming of light. Indeed, it 6 is comparable only to the breaking of dawn; and the gradual influx of divine Light colors the scenes in our mind and dispels one by 9 one the illusions of sense, the darker places in human thought.

The stress of daily living would deprive 12 us of this great Spirit unless we are careful to retire often into the sanctuary of our inner being and there let the Christ be our 15 honored guest.

Never let vain conceit or a belief in personal power keep you from this sacred expe- 18 rience. Be willing. Be receptive. Be still.

SUPPLY

THE SECRET of supply is to be found in Luke 12:22-32.

3 "And he said unto his disciples, Therefore I say unto you, Take no thought for your life, what ye shall eat; neither for the body,

6 what ye shall put on.

"The life is more than meat, and the body is more than raiment.

9 "Consider the ravens; for they neither sow nor reap; which neither have storehouse nor barn; and God feedeth them: how much

12 more are ye better than the fowls?

"And which of you with taking thought can add to his stature one cubit?

15 "If ye then be not able to do that thing which is least, why take ye thought for the rest?

18 "Consider the lilies how they grow; they toil not, they spin not; and yet I say unto you, that Solomon in all his glory was not

21 arrayed like one of these.

"If then God so clothe the grass, which is today in the field, and tomorrow is cast into the oven; how much more will he clothe 3 you, O ye of little faith?

"And seek not ye what ye shall eat, or what ye shall drink, neither be ye of doubt- 6 ful mind.

"For all these things do the nations of the world seek after: and your Father knoweth 9 that ye have need of these things.

"But rather seek ye the kingdom of God; and all these things shall be added unto you. 12

"Fear not, little flock; for it is your Father's good pleasure to give you the kingdom."

15

The question now arises: how is it possible to "take no thought" for money when pressing obligations must be met? How can 18 we trust God when year in and year out these financial problems confront us, and usually through no fault of our own? We have seen 21 in these passages from Luke that the way to solve our difficulties is to take no thought for supply, whether of money, food, cloth- 24 ing or any other form. And the reason that

we need have no anxiety about these things is that "it is your Father's good pleasure to
3 GIVE you the kingdom" because He "knoweth that ye have need of these things."

In order that we may enter wholly into the
6 Spirit of confidence in this inspired message of Scripture, we must understand that money is not supply but is the result or effect
9 of supply. There is no such thing as a supply of money, clothes, homes, automobiles or food. All these constitute the effect of sup-
12 ply and if this infinite supply were not present within you, there never would be the added things" in your experience. The added
15 things, of course, are those practical things like money, food and clothing that are so necessary at this stage of our existence.

18 Since money is not supply, what is? Let us digress for a moment and look at the orange tree which is laden with fruit. We
21 know that the oranges do not constitute supply because when these have been eaten, or sold, or given away, a new crop starts at
24 once to grow. The oranges are gone but the supply remains. Within that tree there is a

law in operation. Call it a law of God or a
law of nature—the name of the law is not
too important, but the recognition of the 3
presence of a law operating in, through or
as the tree—is important. That law operates
to draw in through the roots, the minerals, 6
substances, elements of air, water and sun-
shine which it (the law) then transforms into
sap that is drawn up through the trunk of 9
the tree and distributed through the branches
and finally sent into expression as blossoms.
In due time this law transforms the blossoms 12
into a green marble and this becomes the
full grown orange. The orange is the result
or effect of the operation of the law acting 15
in, through and as the orange tree. As long
as this law is present we will have oranges.
The orange of itself cannot produce an- 18
other orange. Thus we understand that the
law is the supply and oranges are the fruits,
the results or the effect of the law. 21

Within you and within me there is also a
law in operation—a law of life—and our
awareness of the presence of this law is our 24
supply. Money, and the things necessary for

daily living are the effects of the consciousness of the activity of the law within. This
3 understanding enables us to take thought off the things of the outer world and abide in the consciousness of the law.

6 What is the law which is our supply? The universal or divine Consciousness, your individual consciousness, is this law. This law
9 actually is your consciousness. Thus your consciousness becomes the law of supply unto you, producing its own image and likeness
12 in the form of those things necessary to your well being. As there is no limitation to your consciousness, there is no limit to your con-
15 scious awareness of the action of the law and therefore no limit to your supply in all its forms.

18 Divine or universal Consciousness, your individual consciousness, is spiritual. The activity of this law within you is likewise
21 spiritual and therefore your supply in all its forms is spiritual, infinite and everpresent. What we behold as money, food and cloth-
24 ing, automobiles and homes, represents our

concepts of these ideas. Our concepts are as infinite as our Mind.

Let us agree now to see that as we need 3 take no thought for oranges as long as we have the source or supply which is continual- ly producing fruit for us, so we need no 6 longer take thought about dollars. Let us learn to think of dollars as we do of leaves on trees, or oranges, as the natural and in- 9 evitable result of the law active within. There is truly no need to be concerned even when the trees appear to be bare, as 12 long as we are conscious of the truth that the law is even now operating within to bring forth fruit after its own kind. Regard- 15 less of the state of our finances at any given moment, let us not be concerned or worried because we now know that the law acting in, 18 through and as our consciousness, is at work within us, when we are asleep as well as when we are awake, to provide all those 21 added things.

Let us learn to look at the lilies and re- joice at the proof of the presence of God's 24 love for His creation. Let us watch the sparrows and note how confidently they trust this law.

3   Let us rejoice when we see the flowers in Spring and Summer because they assure us of the divine Presence. As we learn to enjoy

6 the beauties and bounties of nature, with no desire to hoard any of them, and with no fear that there is less than an infinite supply

9 of them, so learn to enjoy the fruitage of our infinite supply—the results of that infinite storehouse within us—with no fear of any

12 lack to plague us.

    Enjoy these things of the outer realm but do not consider them as supply. Our con-

15 scious awareness of the presence and activity of the law is our consciousness of supply and the outer things are the forms our con-

18 sciousness takes on. The inner supply appears as the necessary outer things.

SUPPLY

PART II

W E SAY in one breath—take no thought for your supply—or for your health, and in the next breath, we say you must "pray 3 without ceasing" and "ye shall know the truth, and the truth shall make you free." Though seeming to be contradictory, both 6 admonitions are correct, but they have to be understood.

There is always a belief of human good 9 in operation—a law of averages, and from this we derive our material benefit. In house to house selling, there is usually an average 12 of one sale out of twenty calls; in advertising through circulars, there is an average of returns of about 2%; in automobile driving, 15 it is claimed a certain percentage of accidents is the rule; life insurance companies have a table of life expectancy, and they can 18 tell you any year how many years you will continue here—as an average.

Now to live humanly, that is to go along 21

day to day *letting* these averages affect you, letting the human beliefs operate upon you,
3 is not scientific living. This is all the belief of human existence, and unless you specifically do something about it, you bring
6 yourself under these so-called economic or health laws, which actually are but beliefs or suggestions. These suggestions are so uni-
9 versal as to become mesmeric in their operation and act on those who are not alert, and bring forth limitation.

12 What must we do to keep ourselves free of these suggestions, so that we can live above them? First, we must live on a higher
15 plane of consciousness. So far as possible, we must train ourselves mentally to know that anything that exists in the realm of ef-
18 fect is not cause, is not creative, and has no power over us. This brings up the important metaphysical point that I am the law, I am
21 Truth, I am Life eternal. Since I am infinite consciousness, since I am the law, then nothing in the external can act upon
24 me and be a law unto me. There is nothing from which we can ever suffer but the ac-

ceptance of illusion as Reality. These things called sin and disease are not what we are suffering from, they are the forms the one 3 error assumes. Regardless of the name you use, they are hypnotism, suggestion, illusion, appearing as person, place or thing—ap- 6 pearing as sin, disease, lack and limitation.

We must not live as though we were ef- fect with something operating upon us. Let 9 us remember to live as the law, as the Princi- ple of our being. You can only take posses- sion of your affairs as you consciously realize 12 that they are the effect of your own con- sciousness; the image and likeness of your own being; the manifestation or expression 15 of your divine Self—then alone can you be a law unto them.

We must begin our days with the inner 18 reminder of our true identity. We must identify ourselves as Spirit, as Principle, as the law of Life unto our affairs. It is a very 21 necessary thing to remember that we have no needs; we are infinite, individual, spiritual consciousness embodying within ourselves 24 the infinity of good, therefore, we are that

center, that point of God consciousness which can feed five thousand any day and
3 every day,—not by using our bank account, but by using the infinity of good pouring through us the same as it poured through
6 Jesus. We do not meet people with the idea of what we can get or what they can do for us, but we go out into life as the presence
9 of God. During the day, whether doing housework, driving cars, selling or buying, we must consciously remember that we are
12 the law unto our universe and that means that we are a law of Love unto all with whom we come in contact. Consciously re-
15 member that all who come within range of our thought and activity must be blessed by the contact, because we are a law of Love;
18 we are the Light of the world. Consciously remember that we do not need anything, because we are the law of supply in action—
21 we can feed five thousand of those who do not yet know their identity.

There is a belief of separation between us
24 and God—our good—and this we correct by realizing, "I and my Father are one";—"All

that the Father hath is mine";—"the place whereon I stand is holy ground." In the recognition of the infinity of our being, we realize the truth of the Bible; we realize the truth of these promises; they are no longer quotations, but statements of fact, and that brings us to the point of demarcation between "knowing the truth," and "taking no thought." We are realizing truth now as an established truth within our own consciousness—the truth of our being. We are not taking thought to make any good come to us; we are not giving ourselves a treatment to make something happen to us, but we are realizing the truth, knowing the truth of our own identity, of our oneness with the infinite, with our infinite capacities. The reason for realizing and knowing this truth is that through the ages we have come to be known as man—as something other than God-being—and unless we now consciously and daily remind ourselves of the true nature of our being, we will come under the general belief that we are something separate and apart from God.

There is a belief that we are separate from some people who are really a part of our completeness; a belief that we are separate or apart from certain spiritual ideas necessary to our fulfillment, and these may appear as persons, papers, home, companionship, opportunity. This we correct by realizing that our oneness with God constitutes our oneness with every idea. Illustrative of this is the telephone. Through my telephone I can reach any other telephone any place in the world, but I cannot reach even my next door neighbor by telephone without first going through the central station. Then by establishing my oneness with central, I am one with every telephone. In the realization of our oneness with infinite Principle, Love, God, we find and manifest our oneness with every idea necessary to the unfoldment of our completeness.

Never forget that you cannot live scientifically as man or idea, but that you must realize yourself to be Life, Truth and Love. You must accept Jesus' revelation of the I AM until it becomes realization with you.

SUPPLY

Stop trying to apply Truth; applying Truth is the action of the human thought— there is nothing to apply Truth to. Truth is infinite, therefore, there is nothing to which we can apply Truth. It is the reality of being and there is nothing inside or outside for Truth to act upon—Truth is self-acting, self-operative.

We are all engaged in activities through which our supply appears to come. Regardless of whether it is a business, a profession, or an art, it is an activity of Mind and Life. So regarded, our activity is intelligently and lovingly directed and sustained. It is even more than this: As an emanation of Mind, it is Mind itself individually appearing and expressing its own being, nature and character. The government is upon Its shoulder, and Mind alone is responsible. We learn to let go and let Mind assume its responsibilities.

In the Bible we read the trials and tribulations of Elijah. As we follow him through the 18th Chapter of I Kings, we must understand that only the consciousness of the

presence of Spirit, God—within him—could
have done these mighty works. No human
3 power can accomplish them.

In the 19th Chapter, we find discouragement creeping in at what appears as the fail-
6 ure of Elijah's ministry. Actually this is an
opportunity to prove that the power is not
that of a human, but actually is God-power
9 appearing as what appears as a man, but
really is God appearing as an individual.

The food prepared for Elijah under the
12 juniper tree is his own awareness of the
presence of God appearing in tangible form.

We are led in this 19th Chapter of I Kings
15 to the great message in the 18th verse, "Yet
I have left me seven thousand in Israel, all
the knees which have not bowed unto Baal,
18 and every mouth which hath not kissed him."
You note here, that God has not saved
seven thousand for Elijah, but for Himself—
21 for God appearing as Elijah.

Whatever our work may be—in business,
in a profession, or as an artist—God, the
24 Mind of the individual, always has kept
seven thousand (completeness) for Himself,

and as we learn to listen for that still small voice which spoke to Elijah, we too will be led to where our work and recognition and compensation are to be found. You exist as individual Mind, therefore, all that is necessary to your fulfillment is included in the infinite consciousness which you are.

In an individual way, God is expressing Itself as you, and your abilities are really the abilities of God; your activity is actually the activity of Mind, Life; and, therefore, the responsibility for you is God's responsibility. Gain this consciousness of God's presence and you have the whole secret of success in every walk of life.

As individual spiritual consciousness, there are seven thousand (fulfillment) prepared for you—that is, God, the Mind of the individual, the Mind of you, has given you your individual abilities and capacities, and likewise has given you the opportunity and the rewards. These appear to fit each situation.

Always remember that God, the Mind of you, has prepared for you all that is neces-

151

sary for the fulfillment of your individual experience. You are never outside the har-
3 mony of God's being. Cultivate the consciousness of the presence of God every moment.

6 It is our conscious union with God which enables us to live without taking thought and makes possible a life of complete abun-
9 dance—"by Grace."

There is an invisible bond between all of us. We are not on earth to get from one
12 another, but to share the spiritual treasures which are of God. Our interest in each other is, in Truth, purely spiritual. Our purpose
15 in life is the unfolding of the Spirit within.

From the height of spiritual vision we do not look upon each other as man and
18 woman; as rich or poor; as grand or humble. All human values are submerged in our common interest to seek and find the King-
21 dom within. We see each other as travellers on the Path of Light; we share our unfoldments, our experiences, and our spiritual
24 resources. We would not withhold any of

these from each other.

Likewise, there is no envy or jealousy of each other's spiritual attainments. Let us even for a moment realize that whatever we possess of supply, position, prestige or power, health, beauty or wealth, is the gift of God and, therefore, equally available to all of us in the measure of our openness of consciousness—and you understand how we can carry our impersonal love out into the human world.

Let us once catch the vision that whatever anyone possesses, even of what appears as material good, is but the expression of their state of consciousness, and it would be impossible to envy any of another's possessions, or even to desire them. The first step in living by Grace, living in universal peace, must begin with the understanding that all anyone has is of the Father; that is, all that we possess and all that we can ever own is the outpouring of our own infinite consciousness.

We are all "joint heirs with Christ in God", therefore, we all draw upon the re-

sources of our own infinite Mind and Soul,
and we need not labor, strive or struggle
3 for that which is already divinely ours. All
that anyone possesses at any time, even of
what seems to be of human value, is the
6 unfoldment of their own state of consciousness and, therefore, belongs only to the
possessor. That which we have is the result
9 of fruitage of our own state of consciousness,
and what we have not yet achieved, is our
own lack of conscious union with God—our
12 infinite Consciousness.

We can have as much of everything as
we desire by enlarging the borders of our
15 understanding and realization. Nothing that
we can get from another would ever really
be ours, even if we received it legally. It
18 would still belong only to the one with the
consciousness of it. What is yours is eternally
yours and only because it is your state of
21 consciousness in expression.

"All that the Father (my very own infinite
consciousness) hath—is mine."
24 The realization of this Truth would
enable all men to live together in one

world harmoniously, joyously, successfully,
—without fear of each other and without
greed, envy or lust. We would be back in   3
the Garden of Eden. We would live without
taking thought,—which is by Grace. This
would constitute the recognition of life as   6
the gift of God—as the free flow of our
consciousness. It would reveal the invisible
spiritual tie which binds us in an eternal   9
brotherhood of Love. It would forever solve
the problem of supply and thereby establish
the reign of peace on earth.   12

THE NEW HORIZON

THE SENSE which presents pictures of discord and inharmony, disease and death, is the universal mesmerism which produces the entire dream of human existence. It must be understood that there is no more reality to harmonious human existence than to discordant world conditions. It must be realized that the entire human scene is mesmeric suggestion and we must rise above the desire for even good human conditions. Understand fully that suggestion, belief, hypnotism, is the substance or fabric of the whole mortal universe and that human conditions of both good and evil are dream pictures having no reality or permanence. Be willing for the harmonious as well as the inharmonious conditions of mortal existence to disappear from your experience in order that Reality may be known and enjoyed and lived.

Above this sense life there is a universe

of Spirit governed by Love; peopled with children of God living in the household or Temple of Truth. This world is real and permanent. Its substance is eternal consciousness. In it there is no awareness of discords or even of temporary and material good.

The first glimpse of Reality—of the Soul realm—comes with the recognition and realization of the fact that all temporal conditions and experiences are products of self-hypnotism. With the realization that the entire human scene—its good as well as its evil—is illusion, comes the first glimpse and taste of the world of God's creation and of the sons of God who inhabit the spiritual kingdom.

Now, in this moment of uplifted consciousness, we are able, even though faintly, to see ourselves free of material, mortal, human and legal laws. We behold ourselves separate and apart from the bondage of sense and in a measure we glimpse the unlimited boundaries of eternal Life and of infinite Mind. The fetters of finite existence begin to fall away; the price tags start to disappear.

We no longer dwell in thought on human happiness or prosperity nor is there any longer concern about health or home. The "wider, grander view" is coming into focus. The freedom of divine being is becoming apparent.

The experience at first is like watching the world disappear over a horizon and drop down from before us. There is no attachment to this world, no desire to hold on to it—probably because to a great extent the experience does not come until a great measure of our desire for the things of "this world" has been overcome. At first we cannot speak of it. There is a sense of "Touch me not for I have not yet ascended"; "I am still between the two worlds, do not touch me or make me speak of it because it may drag me back. Let me be free to rise; then, when I am completely free of the mesmerism and its pictures, I will tell you of many things which eyes have not seen nor ears heard."

A universal illusion binds us to earth—to temporal conditions. Realize this, understand this, because only through this under-

standing can we begin to lessen its hold upon us. The more fascinated we are with conditions of human good; the greater our 3
desire for even the good things of the flesh, the more intense is the illusion. In proportion as our thought dwells on God, on things 6
of the Spirit, the greater freedom from limitation are we gaining. Think neither on the discords nor on the harmonies of this 9
world. Let us not fear the evil nor love the good of human existence. In proportion as we accomplish this is the mesmeric influence 12
lessening in our experience. Earth ties begin to disappear; shackles of limitation fall away; erroneous conditions give place to 15
spiritual harmony; death gives way to eternal life.

The first glimpse into the heaven of here 18
and now is the beginning of the Ascension for us. This Ascension is understood now as a rising above the conditions and experi- 21
ences of "this world" and we behold the "many mansions" prepared for us in spiritual Consciousness — in the awareness of 24
Reality.

We are not bound by evidence of the

physical senses; we are not limited to the
visible supply; we are not circumscribed by
3 visible bonds or bounds; we are not tied
by visible concepts of time or space. Our
good is flowing from the infinite invisible
6 realm of Spirit, Soul, to our immediate
apprehension. Let us not judge of our good
by the sensible evidence. Out of the tre-
9 mendous resources of our Soul comes the
instant awareness of all that we can utilize
for abundant living. No good thing is with-
12 held from us as we look above the physical
evidence to the great Invisible. Look up.
Look up. The kingdom of heaven is at hand.
15 "I" am breaking the sense of limitation
for you as an evidence of "My" presence and
of "My" influence in your experience. "I"—
18 the I of you—am in the midst of you revealing the harmony and infinity of spiritual
existence. "I"—the I of you—never a per-
21 sonal sense of I—never a person—but the I
of you—am ever with you. Look up.

THE NEW JERUSALEM

"The former things have passed away"
and "all things are become new." "Whereas
I was blind, now I see," and not "through a   3
glass, darkly," but "face to face." Yes, even
in my flesh I have seen God. The hills have
rolled away and there is no more horizon   6
but the light of heaven makes all things
plain.

Long have I sought Thee, oh Jerusalem,   9
but only now have my pilgrim feet touched
the soil of heaven. The waste places are no
more. Fertile lands are before me, the like   12
of which I have never dreamed. Oh truly
"There shall be no night there." The glory
of it shines as the noonday sun. And there   15
is no need of light for God is the light
thereof.

I sit down to rest. In the shade of the   18
trees I rest and find my peace in Thee. Within Thy grace is peace, O Lord. In the world
I was weary—in Thee I have found rest.   21

In the dense forest of words I was lost;
in the letter of Truth was tiredness and fear,
3 but in Thy Spirit only is shade and water
and rest.

How far have I wandered from Thy
6 Spirit, O Tender One and True, how far,
how far. How deeply lost in the maze of
words, words, words. But now am I re-
9 turned and in Thy Spirit shall I ever find my
life, my peace, my strength. Thy Spirit is the
bread of life, finding which I shall never
12 hunger. Thy Spirit is a wellspring of water,
and drinking it I shall never thirst.

As a weary wanderer I have sought Thee,
15 and now my weariness is gone. Thy Spirit
has formed a tent for me and in its cool
shade I linger and peace fills my Soul. Thy
18 presence has filled me with peace. Thy love
has placed before me a feast of Spirit. Yea,
Thy Spirit is my resting place, an oasis in
21 the desert of the letter of Truth.

In Thee will I hide from the noise of
the world of argument; in Thy Conscious-
24 ness find surcease from the noisomeness of
men's tongues. They divide Thy garment, O
Lord of Peace, they quarrel over Thy Word

—yea, until it becomes words and no longer Word.

As a beggar have I sought the new heaven 3 and the new earth and Thou hast made me heir of all.

How shall I stand before Thee but in si- 6 lence. How shall I honor Thee but in the meditation of mine heart.

Praise and thanksgiving Thou seekest not, 9 but the understanding heart Thou receivest.

I will keep silent before Thee. My Soul and my Spirit and my silence shall be Thy 12 dwelling place. Thy Spirit shall fill my meditation and it shall make me and pre- serve me whole. O Thou Tender One and 15 True—I am home in Thee.

CPSIA information can be obtained
at www.ICGtesting.com
Printed in the USA
BVHW070037170519
548582BV00002B/152/P

9 781614 271277